TIU^{N} CHHANG-MIÂ (MINNIE MACKAY, 1860?–1925)

Dr Mark A. Dodge

TIU^{N} CHHANG-MIÂ (MINNIE MACKAY, 1860?–1925)

Life in Taiwan's Contested Colonial Space

The Asian Studies Collection

Collection Editor
Dr Dong Wang

LPp

For 艾莉: Taiwan's most beautiful flower

First published in 2024 by Lived Places Publishing

The authors and editors have made every effort to ensure the accuracy of information contained in this publication, but assume no responsibility for any errors, inaccuracies, inconsistencies and omissions. Likewise, every effort has been made to contact copyright holders. If any copyright material has been reproduced unwittingly and without permission the Publisher will gladly receive information enabling them to rectify any error or omission in subsequent editions.

British Library Cataloguing in Publication Data
A CIP record for this book is available from the British Library

ISBN: 9781915734143 (pbk)
ISBN: 9781915734167 (ePDF)
ISBN: 9781915734150 (ePUB)

The right of Mark A. Dodge to be identified as the Author of this work has been asserted by them in accordance with the Copyright, Design and Patents Act 1988.

Cover design by Fiachra McCarthy
Book design by Rachel Trolove of Twin Trail Design
Typeset by Newgen Publishing UK

Lived Places Publishing
Long Island
New York 11789

www.livedplacespublishing.com

Abstract

This book discovers the overlooked life and enduring influence of Tiu[n] Chhang-miâ (1860?–1925), known to the Canada Presbyterian Church as Minnie Mackay. The story of her life as narrated by the Taiwanese Presbyterian Church is a key to understanding how Taiwan's democracy developed and where it is heading.

Tiu[n] Chhang-miâ (1860?–1925) tells of a Fujian-Taiwanese woman, the first from Taiwan (or the Qing Empire for that matter) to legally marry a Christian missionary. Tiu[n], along with her husband, George Leslie Mackay, became a pioneering figure in the foundation of Taiwanese Christianity and in Canadian-Taiwanese relations in the nineteenth century. This book recounts Tiu[n]'s life from her sale as a child-bride through her rise to become the symbolic heroine leading the push for education for women and local control of Taiwan and the Taiwanese Presbyterian Church.

Taiwanese lives in the nineteenth century were caught between the faltering Qing Dynasty and various other imperial forces eager to challenge each other's claims of sovereignty by establishing colonies of their own. In those tumultuous times, Tiu[n] provided a model of feminine strengths which reinforced Taiwanese and Canadian ideals of new womanhood, and ultimately became an important element in the formation of a distinctly Taiwanese imaginary of modern womanhood. The complex legacy left by Tiu[n] continues to be felt in Taiwan and elsewhere while that island nation fights, like so many other former colonies, to establish its own identity and existential rights in the post-colonial world.

Keywords

Tiuⁿ Chhang-miâ; Minnie Mackay; George Leslie Mackay; missionary; Taiwanese Presbyterian Church; nineteenth century; Canadian–Taiwanese relations; Asian womanhood; Dutch, British, Chinese, and Japanese colonist; biography; Taiwan; colonialism

Contents

List of figures and tables

Learning objectives

Christianity, gender, and democracy

European and American intellectuals began calling themselves "modern" in the nineteenth century. For them, modernity represented the pinnacle of human achievement in science, industry, and government. Asian elites, faced with the superiority of European military and industrial technology, began to engage in a variety of self-strengthening movements aimed at creating distinctive Asian modernities.

- Explain how the lived experience of Tiu^n Chhang-miâ, a pivotal figure in Taiwanese nationalism and Taiwan's Presbyterian Church, has been diversely narrated by different groups at different times.

- Identify how the nineteenth-century introduction of Christianity in Taiwan helped to shape Tiawan's modern identity, and how Tiu^n's life in particular has been mobilized to represent a distinctively Taiwanese modernity.

- Explore the significance and character of Canadian–Taiwanese relations within the context of Taiwan's colonial period.

- Analyze how Taiwan's contested space throughout the colonial and post-colonial era has affected its quest for sovereign statehood, with hope of better understanding its unique autonomous and international position today.

Introduction

Crafting the story of Taiwan

The nineteenth century is often referred to by historians as the "European century" because, despite its being a relatively small peninsula protruding from the northwest corner of Asia, Europeans managed to explore and subjugate other peoples in nearly every other part of the world. By the end of the century Europeans and their descendants controlled nearly 85 per cent of the earth's surface and ruled over most of its human inhabitants. European historians tend to perceive this period as "the long nineteenth century"—an epoch that began with the French Revolution in 1789 and culminated with the outbreak of "Total War" in Europe in 1914, a periodization which accentuates Europe's rise and fall. This periodization highlights the development of democracy and the technological successes (and failures) of the Industrial Revolution, reinforcing themes of the disastrous consequences of a divided Europe.

Historians of the People's Republic of China (PRC) and their political allies, on the other hand, write of a very different era—one they call 百年國恥 (*bainian guochi*): "the century of humiliations". Theirs is also a long century, but it tells a very different story. For these historians, China's nineteenth century began in 1842 with the signing of the first unequal treaty at the end of the Opium War, or perhaps in 1839 at the beginning of that conflict. This century ended in 1949 with Generalissimo Chiang Kai-shek's retreat to Taiwan, and the victory of the Chinese Communist Party (CCP). This periodization adopts the Marxist/Leninist view of history that centers on the growing weakness of the Qing Dynasty and the CCP as the "inevitable" victor. During these years the Qing Dynasty proved incapable of securing its borders first from the British, but soon from the French, Americans, Russians, Germans, Italians, Austro-Hungarians, and ultimately even the Japanese they had long regarded as their "little brother" in Asian politics. Nor could the Qing Dynasty suppress the long series of internal revolts and civil wars within its borders during this period without the assistance of these same foreign powers. This narrative emphasizes the immense human suffering experienced in China, and attributes much of it to greed and foreign (particularly European) aggression ending with the rise of the CCP to power as the single ruling political party in 1949. This narrative celebrates communist ideology and China's ultimate victory over foreign imperialism, but tends to forget that communism itself was an ideological export of Europe to China.

Charles S. Maeir has suggested that it makes more sense in the study of global history to imagine a century beginning in 1860 and ending in the late 1960s or early 1970s, during which the dual political aims of territoriality and state building were nearly ubiquitous throughout the world. Maeir contends that focusing on the processes by which the empires of the previous era transformed into the consolidated nation states that dominate the world today might produce a more coherent and meaningful narrative of modern world history (Maeir, 2000). Maeir cites such examples as the American Civil War, the Meiji Constitution, and the confederation of Germany, Italy, Canada, Mexico, Thailand, and Argentina as important events that support an 1860 beginning and a variety of Cold War conflicts like the Vietnam War and the emergence of new manufacturing economies such as Brazil and the four Asian Tigers, as justification for his endpoint.

I hold that a period beginning in 1860 and ending in the early 1970s is a strong framework for understanding the modern history of Taiwan as well. The year 1860, when a combined British and French military expedition took Peking and ravaged the emperor's summer palace in order to enforce the terms of the Treaty of Tientsin, which ended the second Opium War, was also the year that the first expeditionary survey of Taiwanfoo was conducted by British emissaries guided by Fujianese merchants. Although Taiwan had been a nexus of international trade since as early as the seventeenth century, the arrival of the Sino-British tea industry in 1860 marked a new beginning of Taiwan in the world economy—a significance that culminated in the years after the Second World War and the exile of Chiang Kai-shek and the Republic of China to Taiwan. In the 1960s and 1970s trade-led economic growth averaged more than 7 per cent per year, making Taiwan's economy one of the fastest growing in the world. Taiwan's miraculous growth earned it a reputation as one of the four Asian Tigers. The year 1971 was also the year that the Republic of China, whose government in exile held Taiwan under martial law, ceased to represent the *other* China in international diplomacy. While the world agreed that China was no longer part of Taiwan, even today the leadership of the PRC continues to contend that Taiwan is part of China. Taiwan continues to enjoy de facto statehood, despite recurring military and political threats from the PRC, but international recognition of Taiwan's sovereignty has suffered significantly since the PRC's 1971 induction to the UN.

The year 1860 is also an appropriate beginning for this particular story. The protagonist, Tiuⁿ Chhang-miâ, is said to have been born that year in Taiwan (although this claim has been questioned), not far from the place that first joint British–Chinese expedition found suitable for the establishment of the infrastructure for a local tea trade. The British embassy at Tamsui, founded that year, became the center for all political and economic dealings between the Qing Empire and all of the other foreign powers operating in Taiwan for many years to come. The success Fujian and British merchants achieved in introducing tea cultivation and processing to Taiwan substantially transformed the Taiwanese economy. In the eighteenth and early nineteenth centuries, sugar, produced primarily in lowland regions of southern Taiwan, was the island's chief export, but by the 1880s tea accounted for more than half of Taiwan's exports, and the economic center of the island had shifted from the south to the northern highlands surrounding the area that would grow to become Taipei. The introduction of the tea trade had a direct impact on the life of Tiuⁿ Chhang-miâ, whose family was one of many to take on an early role in the cultivation and processing of tea. Tiuⁿ's life, as we will see, also had a significant effect on the British success in the tea trade. Tiuⁿ and her husband George Leslie Mackay were imagined as a sort of human bridge between the Fujian-Taiwanese community that produced tea and the British merchants who sought to export it. Their family and the church that it founded provided networks of trust that enabled the British and Taiwanese to cooperatively control Taiwan's most valuable industry throughout the Qing Dynasty's rule of Taiwan, and for many years after Japan colonized the island.

Although Tiu^n passed away in 1925, her influence was keenly felt even into the 1970s, when her children and grandchildren continued to maintain high positions within the Presbyterian Church of Taiwan (PCT), and the PCT continued to play an important role in supporting Taiwan's relationships with countries of the West. Most foreigners, along with many of Tiu^n's direct descendants, were forced to leave Taiwan by 1937 as Japan mobilized the island for war production, and did not return until well after the war was concluded. The Presbyterian Church USA arrived in 1949, with the American military complex that helped support the establishment of the Republic of China in Taiwan. Chiang Kai-shek established martial law throughout Taiwan shortly after his arrival, and the policy continued for thirty-eight years (1949–1987) in what many of the Taiwanese call his "Second White Terror" (the first being the mass exterminations of Chinese Communists and other left-wing radicals in Shanghai, Changsha, and other places in 1927). In 1971, Chiang expelled most foreign missionaries when the PCT and other missionary groups supported UN resolution 2758 to recognize the CCP's rule of China. The PCT was part of a coalition of Christian churches that fought to limit Chiang's international recognition and have Chiang Kai-shek removed from power.

> …to restore all its rights to the People's Republic of China
> and to recognize the representatives of its Government
> as the only legitimate representatives of China to the
> United Nations, and to expel forthwith the represent-
> atives of Chiang Kai-shek from the place which they
> unlawfully occupy at the United Nations and in all the
> organizations related to it.
>
> (1971 UN Resolution 2758)

The PCT subsequently released its "Statement on our National Fate", confirming the church's position on human rights, social responsibility, and self-determination, and begged for support from the international community to establish free elections through which the people of Taiwan could enact their sovereign will in replacing the autocratic regime that had been imposed upon them as a result of the Chinese Civil War. Based on the claim that religious institutions had an obligation to become involved in political affairs when "the Church's life and human rights are violated, then (i) the Church cannot but contend vigorously for the truth of the Gospel and its own life, and (ii) also fight to pro-tect God-given human rights", the PCT issued a statement urg-ing the leadership of Taiwan and the international community to support the introduction of free elections in Taiwan, and to resist a transfer of Taiwan to the control of the PRC (Liu and Kao, 1972).

In 1977, the PCT and its mother church, the Canada Presbyterian Church, once again rose to the forefront of Taiwanese politics by releasing a declaration of human rights that became a founda-tional document in the creation of Taiwanese democracy. The declaration stated:

> As we face the possibility of an invasion by Communist
> China we hold firmly to our faith and to the principles
> underlying the United Nations Universal Declaration of
> Human Rights. We insist that the future of Taiwan shall
> be determined by the seventeen million people who
> live there. We appeal to the countries concerned—espe-
> cially to the people of government of the United States
> of America—and to Christian churches throughout the
> world to take effective steps to support our cause.
>
> (PCT Declaration of Human Rights, August 16, 1977)

Chiang's government in Taiwan imprisoned at least one of the
authors of these foundational documents in the development
of Taiwanese democracy during the Second White Terror in an
attempt to prevent these sentiments from being released to the
international community.

But the political history of Taiwan's long-contested sovereignty is
merely the backdrop of the story I hope to tell here. My intent is
to focus on the life of one Taiwanese woman, Tiuⁿ Chhang-miâ,
and how that life reflected and affected the growing sense of
Taiwanese identity that began to emerge in the late nineteenth
century.

Jane Lee, who has written the most comprehensive Chinese-
language biography of Tiuⁿ Chhang-miâ, claimed that Tiuⁿ's life has
been mobilized as a symbol by many different people at different
times to represent widely divergent values. Tiuⁿ has simultaneously
been characterized as a mere tool used by a foreign missionary to
penetrate the most inaccessible parts of Chinese society, the inner
quarters where women and children resided, and as the "spiritual

mother" (靈性母) of the PCT (Lee, 2014, 9). To many Taiwanese Tiuⁿ's tale was a classic Cinderella story in which a poor local girl was rescued by her marriage to a prominent foreigner and granted a breathtakingly cosmopolitan life in the process. To their Canadian contemporaries, Tiuⁿ represented a model of Christian womanhood, her life demonstrating the transformative power that the Gospels could bestow on oppressed women everywhere. She has been portrayed both as a model of Christian motherhood and as a proto-typical "new woman" venturing out from the inner realm of women to become a leader in the outer world of men, while in Taiwan, she represented radical racial equality. To post-colonial scholars, and par-ticularly those who challenge China's intent to incorporate Taiwan into its growing empire, she has come to represent indigenous challenge to colonial hierarchies and the possibility of a uniquely Taiwanese modernity.

For me, what drew me to this study was the rags-to-riches nar-rative of the young girl, Tiuⁿ, from rural Taiwan who was able to support and eventually manumit herself though her own studies and subsequently rose to become the first head matron of the first school for girls ever constructed in Taiwan, even teaching classes at Oxford College eight years before the first woman was employed to teach at a college in Canada and nearly four dec-ades before a woman was allowed to teach at this high level in China (Wang, 2007). But although the imaginary of the local girl who single-handedly fought to forge her own vision of modern womanhood, despite the multiple overlapping social systems collaborating to prevent her self-empowerment, was deeply alluring to me, the deeper I delved into the scant records of Tiuⁿ's lived life, the more I came to doubt that the reasons Tiuⁿ's life was so significant to me were really reflective of her life at all, or whether any of the narratives of her life reflected her life or simply the ideals of the people who embraced them.

Paul Cohen explains this disconnect between the work of historians, the experiences of people, and the meanings people ascribe to the past by distinguishing three different visions of history: history as event, experience, and myth (Cohen, 1997). Cohen contends that history as experienced by people is inherently messy, filled with contradictory claims in part because of the limited perspective of human participants and in part because of the innate biases they bring to that perspective. Historians who enjoy access to a wider range of perspectives, as well as a distant vantage point by which to better assess the long-term significance of historical events, are naturally able to produce a more balanced and consistent understanding of an event. Mythologizers too produce more cohesive understandings of the past than people who experience it, but often have little to do with people's lived experience of those events. Historians' work differs from that of mythologizers by their careful attention to documenting the experience of an event's participants and their careful assessment of the known facts in their determination of the meaning of an event. While this trichotomy is extremely helpful in navigating and synthesizing the often-contradictory narratives that inevitably emerge around any historical person or event, I will argue that these categories are not as mutually exclusive as Cohen and most historians would like to believe. People mythologize their lives even as they experience them (perhaps before they experience them), and myths often incorporate the same facts upon which more balanced, scholarly, history is founded.

Over the course of this work, in examining the ways that the people and events in northern Taiwan during the late nineteenth and early twentieth centuries have been mobilized to form narratives and those narratives have in turn been woven into distinct social imaginaries, I hope to show that all people employ some combination of these three methodologies in assigning meaning to their experience. I will also try to show that nineteenth-century Taiwan provided a unique set of circumstances that enabled the life of this one woman to represent a wide range of distinct but powerful historic and mythic meanings to some very different groups of people at the same time.

1
Taiwan

A contested colonial space

It is ironic that Formosa, the name given Taiwan by Portuguese conquistadors who landed there in 1590 searching for new lands to colonize and enslave, has come to be associated in recent years with anti-colonialist calls for independence. The fact that the PCT—itself a legacy of foreign intervention on the island—has maintained a leading voice in Taiwan's nationalist movement, despite its relatively slight demographic significance, is similarly surprising (Copper, 2014, 83). Taiwan's rejection of the Chinese empire while simultaneously courting that of the British is counter-intuitive to most students of post-coloniality and is the product of diverse peoples' attempts to construct a meaningful unifying identity in Taiwan despite the existence of multiple competing "modernities". This role-reversal also speaks to the relative effectiveness of the assimilative strategies employed by the Canada Presbyterian Mission with those of other empires within the contested colonial space of Taiwan.

Taiwan has indeed been a contested space almost as long as it has been known to people. Archeological evidence suggests that the island has been inhabited for as many as 30,000 years (Copper, 2014, 31). There is some evidence that there were early migrations to northern Taiwan from China, but the linguistic and cultural ties between the island and Malaysia, Indonesia, and other places in Southeast Asia appear stronger (Hung, 2000, 5–9). In modern times, successive waves of warfare against the indigenous peoples of Taiwan have destroyed much of what was created by these early peoples. Today, the collection of artifacts that was donated to the Royal Ontario Museum by the Canada Presbyterian Mission is believed to be the largest extant collection of Taiwanese indigenous artifacts in the world. There have been some efforts to repatriate this collection in the past, but the bulk of the collection continues to reside at the Royal Ontario Museum in Toronto, Ontario. In 2001 through 2002, much of the collection was displayed at the Shun Ye museum in Taipei as part of a celebration of the life and work of George Leslie Mackay, but political uncertainties and technological limitations continue to delay the collection's permanent return home (Mitchell, 2001).

Records of Chinese explorations of Taiwan in the Sui, Tang, and Song Dynasties prove that China was aware of Taiwan from very early times but did not settle the island. Stories of Japanese fishing vessels running aground on Taiwan, on the other hand, present the likelihood of limited Japanese settlement, but no official contact or recognition (Hung, 2000, 11–16). There may also have been Yuan and Filipino expeditions to the island, but it is doubtful that any of these groups enjoyed more than limited local control. These scattered accounts have been employed separately at various points in history to advance claims of sovereignty over the island, but until fairly recently, Taiwan was an isolated frontier just beyond the control of the great civilizations that surrounded it.

The earliest known name for the island was Pekendo, from the Malayan language (Mackay, 1900, 47). In 1430 the Chinese named its two northern harbors Ke-lung Shan (基隆山) and Taiwan (臺灣), which mean "the thriving base of the great mountain" and "terraced harbor" respectively. The Portuguese called it Ilha Formosa, "the beautiful island", the name that Tiuⁿ Chhang-miâ (張聰明—the subject of our story) used during her lifetime, and that many advocates for Taiwanese independence still use today (Copper, 2014/1975, 7).

In 1624, Taiwan became the subject of international agreement for the first time. Dutch traders of the Vereenigde Oost-Idische Compagnie (VOC or Dutch East India Company) attempted to establish trade with Ming China (1368–1644) in 1604 but had been stopped from landing on the mainland by a fleet of imperial war junks. Three years later, the Ming government allowed the VOC to lay over at the Pescadores Islands off the west coast of Taiwan to set up a trading station. Subsequently the Ming agreed to allow the Dutch to build a more permanent factory for trading on the island of Taiwan. The Dutch declined at the time but returned in 1622 and built a twenty-gun fortress in the Pescadores from whence they began raiding villages along the Ming China coast. In June 1624, the Ming navy, under the command of Yu Zigao (俞諮皋), defeated the Dutch at the Pescadores. Yu nevertheless helped the Dutch dismantle their fort and move it to Taiwan, where it was reconstructed near the present-day town of Anping (Hung, 2000, 19–21). This site became known as the Dutch colony of Zeelandia, and Dutch sovereignty there was recognized by Ming China, if not by the other European powers or the island's own inhabitants.

The Dutch claim did not go long uncontested. Don Antonio Carreño de Valdes, eyeing the profitable trade made by the Dutch in the region, led a Spanish fleet to northern Taiwan in May of 1626. The Spanish renamed the island San Salvador and built Fort Santo Domingo at the mouth of the Tamkang river near present-day Tamsui. The following summer, the Spanish launched an attack against their Dutch neighbors, part of an ongoing campaign to reestablish Habsburg control of the Netherlands. The invasion was turned back by a typhoon, but not forgotten. In 1641, as Spain's position deteriorated in Europe (Portuguese independence was formalized earlier that year), the Dutch invaded San Salvador in the wake of an indigenous Pe-po Hoan revolt. Santo Domingo, the Spanish fort at Tamsui, fell in August of 1642 (Hung, 2000, 23–25).

The Dutch control of Taiwan was short lived. Within two years, the Ming fell to Manchu invaders from the north. The Dutch attempted to maintain neutrality in the Ming–Qing conflict, but when the Ming position on the mainland deteriorated, they moved their forces to Taiwan as a final holdout (Andrade, 2005, 8, 31–37).

Tiuⁿ's husband claimed that the indigenous people of Taiwan remembered Dutch rule more fondly than that of the Spanish or the Chinese (Mackay, 1900, 213–214, 268). Whether true or imagined, the Taiwanese love of the Dutch was not reciprocated. The Dutch found the natives to be unruly, unmanageable, and impervious to training. They actively encouraged the immigration of Chinese farmers and craftsmen to Taiwan to build the economic bases for their trading stations at Zeelandia and Tamsui (Copper, 2014/1975, 13–14).

"Chinese" and "China" are problematic terms here. In the seventeenth through nineteenth centuries European observers usually used Chinese to describe their own foreign perception of "racial" identity at odds with the lived realities of the people thus classified. Even today, we tend to perceive of China as a large multi-ethnic state, and call everybody from within its geographic boundaries "Chinese" regardless of their specific backgrounds, which may involve diverse national, ethnic, and linguistic identities. Here local people's ways of identifying themselves shall accordingly be honored as much as possible, placing "Chinese" in inverted commas to, where appropriate, highlight potential ambiguity.

The "Chinese" people that the Dutch encouraged to immigrate to Taiwan were primarily Fujian people from the coastal region around Xiamen (then called Amoy) along the southern coast of China. These settlers were nominally loyal to the failing Ming Dynasty, and after 1644 to the Ming loyalist army led by Koxinga (鄭成功) that resisted the rising Manchu state of the Qing. They brought with them the Fujian (or Hokkien) dialect, the linguistic ancestor of contemporary Taiwanese, as well as many of the cultural artifacts of the Ming Dynasty, including language, religious rites, and fishing and farming techniques, to name a few (Copper 2014/1975, 15). The Dutch greatly appreciated these "Hoklo", which significantly increased the economic viability of the colony and made it a much more stable location from which to conduct trade. As Governor Nicolaes Verburg put it, "The Chinese are the only bees on Formosa that give honey" (Andrade, 2005, ch. 8, 1).

Extracting this honey required the implementation of taxes. These taxes caused significant disaffection among the Chinese inhabitants of Dutch Taiwan and were probably a contributing factor in several uprisings including the 1652 revolt led by Kuo Huai-yi (郭懷一) that resulted in the slaughter of more than four thousand pro-Dutch natives (Hung, 2000, 33). Periodic uprisings against foreign powers and their native sympathizers remained a recurring motif in Taiwanese history through the first half of the twentieth century.

It was a combination of the Dutch response to the Kuo revolt, and Koxinga's weakening position on the mainland that brought the last vestiges of the Ming Dynasty to Taiwan. Kuo had served under Koxinga's father Cheng Chih-lung (鄭芝龍, Zheng Zhilong) and believed that Koxinga would come to his aid and support the overthrow of the Dutch. Over the course of the rebellion nearly 10 per cent of the Chinese population of Taiwan was killed. Afterward, the Dutch enacted many restrictive laws to prevent future uprisings. The Dutch also negotiated a trade treaty with the Qing, which expanded their power in Taiwan at the same time as it prompted the animosity of Ming loyalists. In July 1661, Koxinga, the last great warlord to maintain loyalty to the Ming Dynasty, laid siege to the fort at Zeelandia in a move to take Taiwan from the Dutch. The result was a blood bath. The Dutch only managed to fire two volleys before they were overwhelmed and surrendered. The survivors were allowed to leave in peace (Andrade, 2005, 18, 14–45). Zeelandia became Anping (安平) and Taiwan became the last refuge of the dying Ming Empire.

Koxinga's twenty-year reign may have partially unified and Sinicized Taiwan but Koxinga's new "Chinese" Taiwanese culture was overtly anti-Qing. He expanded the economy and oversaw trade with Japan and Spain and financed the construction of a Confucian temple and academy at Anping that oversaw a Ming-style examination system to support a Taiwanese bureaucracy. Although the Qing never settled a peace with Koxinga or recognized his de facto rule over Taiwan, the Kangxi emperor waited until the death of Koxinga's heir, Zheng Jing, before ordering an invasion of Taiwan in 1681 (Hung, 2000, 64, 105–119).

The incorporation of Taiwan into Qing China, ironically, somewhat reversed the Sinicizing process Koxinga and Zheng's rule had begun. For one thing, the Qing established a military (green banner) post to govern the island, introducing numerous Hakkas and other non-Fujian ethnic "Chinese"/"Hans" to Taiwan and a new layer of ethnic tension to an already volatile cultural mix. Today many scholars trace ongoing ethnic tensions between the Mandarin-speaking Han and Minnan (Hokkien or Taiwanese) speakers to the mass immigration of Guomindang (KMT) loyalists in 1949 when the last vestiges of the Republic of China (ROC)'s government sought refuge in Taiwan, and the subsequent establishment of Mandarin as Taiwan's official language; but this relatively recent event merely exacerbated the ethno-linguistic identification of divergent loyalties that had dominated Taiwan since the late seventeenth century.

Far from establishing a more "Chinese" Taiwan, the Qing actually sought to de-Sinicize the island. Most of the Chinese living in Taiwan when the Qing took over were Fujian Ming loyalists. Unifying and strengthening this population only increased the danger of renewed rebellion. Immigration to Taiwan was henceforth strictly limited, and resident soldiers and Qing officials were required to leave their families behind when taking posts in

Taiwan in hopes of maintaining a high degree of cultural separation between Qing soldiers and officials and the early Hokkien
migrant population in Taiwan (Hung, 2000, 126–130). These seg-
regationist policies were exacerbated by regular periods of military conflict. During the first century of the Qing rule, the Qing
documented the suppression of sixty-five riots and forty larger-
scale armed insurrections. Furthermore, the Qing initiated twelve
wars of their own against the indigenous tribes of the island, in
their attempts to enforce Qing sovereignty (Hung, 2000, 132–
137). By the time the port of Taiwanfoo was opened to British
trade by the Convention of Peking in 1860, Taiwan already had a
250-year history as a contested colonial space.

2
Womanhood in nineteenth-century Taiwan

In the introduction to his groundbreaking work *Orientalism*, Edward Said defined Orientalism as "a western style for dominating, restructuring, and having authority over the Orient… by which European culture was able to manage—and even produce—the Orient politically, sociologically, militarily, ideologically, scientifically, and imaginatively during the post-enlightenment period" (Said, 1978/2014, 3). According to Said, European othering of Asian (and African) societies was an important factor in the mythological genesis of a distinctive European identity, as well as a rhetorical and epistemological tool employed to construct global hierarchies of race, culture, and knowledge which intrinsically subjugated oriental peoples, cultures, and ideals to "Western" ones.

Feminism, both in Europe and Asia, was born within the context of European colonialism, and this process of "orientalizing" Asia. Liu, Karl, and Ko point out that "progressive thinkers—and educated Asian men in general—were confronted on the one hand with the assault on their self-image as men by the hypermasculinity of the military powers of Western colonialism and imperialism; on the other hand, they were bombarded with accusations of their enslavement of women—foot-binding, concubinage, and sati being cited as chief examples—which became one important moral justification for the imperialist assault on societies classified as 'barbarous' and 'half-civilized' (Liu, Karl, and Ko, 2013, 6). At the same time, Ghosh finds it ironic that British female feminists in colonial contexts often found it more advantageous to embrace inequitable gendered roles in support of racial and cultural hierarchies which empowered white women and elevated them to a leisurely class (Ghosh, 2004, 721–722).

These ideological biases profoundly influenced the earliest studies of women's history in Asia and have been incorporated into the analytic framework for Asian gender studies ever since. Ko contends that "so powerful is this coalescence of Western and Chinese discourses that even Chinese scholars critical of the Orientalist lapses of Western writers are just as committed to the view of Chinese Women's history as a "a history of enslavement," and that it amounts to the "invention of an ahistorical 'Chinese tradition' that is feudal, patriarchal, and oppressive" (Ko, 1994, 3). Ko places much of the blame for this particular mythologization of Asia's past upon the May Fourth movement, and the proliferation of the Chinese Communist Party's subsequent pro/post-modernist agenda, but the roots of this "traditional Chinese patriarchal society" mystique are clearly in the Western colonial critiques intent on undermining the authority of pre-colonial social structures in East Asia. On the other hand, Western condemnations of East Asian norms were not based on biases alone, but upon observations of real conditions experienced by women throughout Asia. These observed conditions were juxtaposed and collated into a unified narrative that justified foreign intervention, even before Tiuⁿ Chhang-miâ, the focus of this narrative, was born. The new womanhood that Tiuⁿ's life would come to represent already existed as an imagined ideal before she embodied it.

Tiuⁿ was born in the small agrarian village of Go Kho-khiⁿ (五故坑) just north of Taipei and grew up to become an international celebrity. Her husband, the Canadian missionary George Leslie Mackay, is often described as the most successful Protestant missionary in the nineteenth century, due to the number of schools, hospitals, and churches built, and people who converted to Christianity to follow him. His success, in turn, is often attributed in Taiwan to the popularity of his wife. Despite her humble beginnings, Tiuⁿ became the first person from Taiwan to travel around the world, the first Taiwanese woman to teach in a college, and the first head matron of the first school for girls ever built in Taiwan. In Taiwan she is considered the mother of the Taiwanese Presbyterian Church , an organization which has strongly influenced the construction of modern Taiwanese democracy and identity.

Tiuⁿ accomplished all of these things despite growing up in the notorious "traditional patriarchal society" that pervaded the late Qing Dynasty. The lives of Taiwanese women were precarious in many ways. Devoid of legal rights and greatly restricted in their ability to generate and control economic resources, many women in late imperial Taiwan lived lives comparable to those of enslaved persons. Taiwanese women were subjected to the threats of selective infanticide, foot-binding, minor marriage, concubinage, and bonded servitude. In most of East Asia, intermingling of the sexes outside of family bonds was deeply frowned upon, and in Qing China in particular the world was strictly divided into two gendered spheres according to the sensibility of *nanwainünei* (男外女內—men outer, women inner), which dictated that the proper role for women was to manage the sphere inside the family home, while men were responsible for dealing with the world outside. The strict segregation of sexes meant that many women spent most of their lifetimes sequestered within their family home.

The majority of these women were not listed in their birth family's genealogy as they ceased being part of their original family once married. While they would forever owe the obligations of filiality to their new family, only those who gave birth to male children would have their names recorded on this family's spirit tablets. It is likely that many women lived whole lifetimes without ever being known outside of their families' households, and without ever having their life recorded or remembered in any way.

Tiuⁿ's birthmother, for example, was known as Ai Si (愛氏), which means the loved woman of the household. Her name is recorded on the Tiuⁿ (張) family ancestor tablets because she mothered three sons. The only other place her name was recorded was on the marriage contract signed by her and her husband granting their daughter's marriage to George Leslie Mackay, which was itself an anomaly arising out of Mackay's attempt to adhere to two very different sets of wedding conventions simultaneously. By contrast, several pages were devoted to Tiuⁿ Chhang-miâ in her birthparents' genealogy, despite the fact that she was transferred to another family at a young age. Tiuⁿ's inclusion is mainly due to her subsequent fame, and she continues to be the only woman significantly identified in the Zhang family's 350-year history in Taiwan.

According to her nephew Zhang Yuehan (see Further Reading), Tiuⁿ Chhang-miâ was known as Chhang-a (蔥仔) or "little scallion" when she was young. Later, when she became famous as a "new woman", single-handedly fighting to overthrow generations of oppressive social conventions, many came to imagine that she had earned the nickname "scallion" because of her feisty personality and her determination to challenge conventional authority and assert her individual rights, but again, she was a scallion long before she was old enough to act like one. The true origin of her nickname lay in the then common Taiwanese practice of naming children after pungent and less tasty foods in the hope that the evil spirits that devoured young children might be scared away by such a foul-sounding name and inadvertently spare those children. There were, after all, plenty of evil spirits around to gobble up small kids in nineteenth-century Taiwan. Malaria, for one, was responsible for the death of more than 20 per cent of Taiwanese-born children before the age of five (Shepherd, 2011, 52–53). Influenza, meningitis, tuberculosis, dysentery, cholera, and multiple varieties of venomous snakes were all endemic child-killers in nineteenth-century Taiwan.

Reliable data concerning overall infant mortality trends in Taiwan does not exist prior to the introduction of a census by the Japanese in 1904. For that year, Shepherd estimates it to have been about 30 per cent (Shepherd, 2011, 50), but it seems likely that in the nineteenth century, prior to the arrival of quinine and widespread mosquito eradication and sanitation control projects of the 1890s, that infant mortality exceeded 40 per cent by the age of five. Taiwanese parents (like parents everywhere in this premodern moment) had to be inured to the fact that many of their children would not live to adulthood, and perhaps they named them accordingly. Many people assumed other (often homonymous) names later during adulthood, and Tiuⁿ was one of these. Her future husband, George Leslie Mackay, renamed her Chhang-miâ (聰明), which meant brilliant, at her baptism when she was eighteen *sui*. No longer would she be remembered simply for her contentiousness, but for her formidable intellect as well.

In addition to these indiscriminate demons that claimed the lives of children in the form of disease, Taiwan had a human malady that specifically targeted female children—infanticide or *ninü* (溺女). Sex-selective infanticide was practiced in many parts of the world in premodern times, and still appears in the form of the high prevalence of sex-selective abortions in the PRC especially during the 1970s–2000s and other parts of the world today, but in the missionary movement of the nineteenth century, the practice of female infanticide was described as a particularly Chinese (and in this case Taiwanese) practice, and a compelling motive for foreign intervention in the region. Saving girls from being thrown away became one of the focal points of Protestant missionary activities in China, and a gripping sentimentalist narrative for rallying the economic and political support of Western Christians for colonial interventions there. Elsie Singmaster, the first anglophone biographer of Tiuⁿ Chhang-miâ, reported that her parents debated for several days whether to allow the child to live or not. Her description of sex-selective infanticide was typical of Western orientalist critiques of this period:

> When a daughter is born, little notice is taken of the event. If she should be deformed in any way, such as having a harelip, she may be immediately destroyed. If the parents already have girls, and are poor, even though it costs the mother a terrible struggle—for the maternal instinct cannot easily be eradicated—the child must sooner or later be put out of the way. As the struggle for life is hard and keen, the sooner the unwelcome baby girl is sacrificed the better.
>
> (Singmaster, 1930, 131–133)

Early Western observers pointed to infanticide as evidence of the moral deficiency of the Chinese, and in their descriptions of the practice often embellished it to make it appear as horrific and as ubiquitous as possible. One of Britain's first visitors to Taiwan, William Pickering, wrote that female infanticide was universally practiced. In his book, he recounted the explanation of one widow he had met:

> 'Oh we all do it about here,' she replied. 'We don't kill the boys, of course; but girls are a lot of trouble, and very little good. You see, if we have one girl after another, and they are not very pretty, we can't get husbands for them, so they are left on our hands. We don't like to sell them for slaves, or to lead a bad life, and so'—she sighed—'we choke them before they know where they are and they don't feel anything.'
>
> (Pickering, 1898, 58–61)

Lee and Feng's landmark book on Chinese infanticide claims that the practice was uncommon in Taiwan (Lee and Feng, 1999, 47) but Michelle King disagrees. According to King, Fujian province (including Taiwan and the mainland home from whence most ethnic Han living in Taiwan came) accounted for as many as half of all confirmed cases of female infanticide in early-modern China. She argues that having an elder male at the head of each Confucian family was so important to the maintenance of family harmony that many families routinely euthanized daughters that were born without an older male sibling. Furthermore, King argues that poverty and hardship often caused families to make similar decisions for later children as well, and girls, who had fewer opportunities to contribute to the family economy, were far more likely to be euthanized than their male siblings (King, 2014, 17–46). Lee and Feng concur that fertility trends within the households of lesser noble families throughout mainland China seem to exhibit a pattern that favors first-born males and that the longer birth intervals following male births among families of this social class may be indicative of differences in marital restraint as well as the duration and quality of postnatal care, but find that in the most impoverished households, the largest gender ratio is not among first-born children, but among the last born, of which nearly 80 per cent were found to be male. Lee and Feng interpret this to mean that poorer families often stopped having children (whether through marital restraint or infanticide) once a son had been born. Since many of these families had several female children in addition to this single male heir, it seems that having a first-born male heir was not as important to peasant families as stopping raising children once that male heir was born (Lee and Feng, 1999, 89, 98–99). In these lower-status families it seems that, if infanticide was indeed the primary vehicle of fertility control, the impetus for infanticide was probably much less gender-specific.

Kelly Olds used data from Japanese censuses to calculate the specific rates of excess female mortality for girls born during the last few decades of Qing rule in Taiwan, to determine how prevalent the practice of female infanticide may have been. He found the excess female mortality dropped from a high of about 5.5 per cent to 1.5 per cent in the years directly following Japan's 1895 takeover and suggested that an increase in the potential economic value of female labor under Japanese rule led to a decrease in female infant mortality (Olds, 2006, 206–221). While Japanese societies also have long histories of infanticide, there was a strong push in Meiji Japan to suppress the practice in order to increase the population as an empire-building resource. They extended this policy to their first colony for similar reasons. Certainly, there was an increase in the availability of wage labor positions open to "new women" outside their homes in both Japan and Taiwan at the end of the nineteenth and beginning of the twentieth century, but the fact that there were early-modern economic factors that contributed to the decline of sex-selective infanticide does not prove that the practice was extensive before those factors emerged.

The records we have indicate that there was a measurable difference between the male and female populations in early-modern Taiwan, but that difference cannot necessarily be solely attributed to female infanticide. Qing soldiers and bureaucrats stationed in Taiwan, for example, were not allowed to bring their female family with them. There were also large numbers of male migratory laborers in late nineteenth-century Taiwan seeking employment in the growing tea industry. Both of these migratory patterns resulted in enlarged populations of adult males in Taiwan. This immigration pattern resulted in the replacement of male children lost to childhood diseases with older male migrants, creating the illusion that the male children had grown up normally and become adult members of Taiwanese society. Meanwhile, female children lost during childhood were not replaced by immigrants from the mainland, resulting in a significant decrease in the female adult population which many have interpreted as evidence of elevated excess female mortality rates. Moreover, if any of these male immigrants married while in Taiwan and later re-emigrated with their spouse and children to the mainland, it would further reduce the later adult female population and could cause the appearance of excess female mortality. The fact that most Taiwanese women lived their lives anonymously sequestered in their family home makes determining whether women died or moved or simply continued to live within their household outside of the written record almost impossible.

Still, it is clear from the multiplicity of anecdotes that infanticide was not *unknown* in Taiwan and that it affected females more frequently than it did males. According to Olds, the difference in male and female infant mortality may have been as high as 10 per cent in the late nineteenth century. If all these excess deaths were directly attributable to sex-selective infanticide (and other more innocuous forms of gender-specific childhood neglect), it would mean one out of every ten female births was subjected to infanticide. But if we assume normal gender ratios (1.02 boys per girl born) and fertility rates (6.5 births per woman), approximately one out of every six and a half female births would be a first-born girl. If every family practiced sex-selective infanticide as Pickering described it, then nearly 16 per cent of all female births would have resulted in infanticide, which would have resulted in an 19.04 per cent increase in excess female infant mortality (nearly twice as much as Olds had demonstrated). When combined with the unbalanced gender ratios of subsequent immigration, it becomes clear that the practice of female infanticide was not as widespread as early Western observers (or even Michelle King) claimed it to be. But even if the true excess female infant mortality were a mere 5 per cent or less, it would still mean that one out of every twenty girls born in Taiwan died during infancy either by drowning or neglect merely because she had been born without an older brother to maintain family harmony.

Although Singmaster emphasized the drawn-out deliberations during which her family decided to allow Tiuⁿ to live, there appears to be little basis for this claim other than the cultural biases of the author. Neither the Tiuⁿ family genealogy nor the ten-page history of the early church written by her nephew, Zhang Yuehan—the only two first-hand accounts of Tiuⁿ's childhood—mentions the alleged proposal of infanticide. On the contrary, both indicate that Tiuⁿ's father welcomed her birth as an opportunity to advance the family's prestige by marrying her to the future son of his cousin who had recently married the younger brother of the village headman—a member of the wealthy Tan clan. Tiuⁿ also came from a family of some means and had an older brother, two facts which theoretically would have helped protect her from this fate.

But even if Tiuⁿ's birth rank had been disadvantageous or her family were struggling with poverty, the decision of whether or not to raise Tiuⁿ to adulthood surely would not have been made the way Singmaster portrayed it—by a stern and detached father against the pleading cries of a feeble but loving mother. King shows that the vast majority of Chinese language sources place the responsibility for decisions concerning infanticide on the women (female relatives and hired midwifes) present in the birthing room, a place where men were generally excluded. In the context of polygamous multi-generational households, where every child presented the possibility of altering the often-delicate balance of family politics, the motivation to euthanize an infant female often had as much to do with the implications her birth had for the relative statuses of the mother and the other women involved as economic considerations. During such discussions, it was more often the men of the family who attempted to intervene to prevent infanticide (King, 2014, 29–34). Of course, the imaginaries based upon Fujian gender biases are just as much to play as Singmaster's Western feminist biases are in the construction of these divergent narratives. The choice to portray women as cold, conniving competitors is mobilized in these narratives to promote a strong and benevolent outlook among male heads of family just as the pleading mother trying to protect her dearly loved daughter hopes to promote a specific brand of maternal commitment among women in the narratives of the West. While both of these archetypal figures undoubtedly existed among the tens of thousands of families that found themselves making this choice, it is clear that neither archetype was as pervasive as the authors who chose to idolize them hoped they would be.

Tiu^n was reported (by a Western newspaper) to have told an audience at Woodstock's Knox Church in 1880 that her mother attempted to kill her by smothering her between blankets when she was young, and after that she went to live with her grand-father for seven years (*Sentinel Review*, July 16, 1880). As she was touring Canada with her husband and speaking at many churches that year, it is likely that she told some version of this same story dozens of other times as well. Singmaster may have derived her infanticide narrative in part from these accounts, but this event was not an attempted infanticide, but rather a very for-cibly failed assisted suicide. According to her nephew's account, Tiu^n was twelve *sui* when she went to live with her grandpar-ents (Zhang, 1987, 1). If the story of smothering was based on a true event, it would not have been her *birth*mother that tried to smother her as an infant, but her adoptive mother or *yangmu* (養母) who tried to kill her when she was ten or eleven years old. The facts that Tiu^n had been raised outside of her birth family as a child-bride and that she had been widowed at the young age of ten or eleven were omitted from the Canadian reports, which perhaps contributed to Singmaster's understanding. Tiu^n's knowledge of English was minimal at the time, and her speeches were translated by her husband, himself a missionary, invested in the transformative possibilities of the orientalist narrative, so there are many reasons why the story came about the way it did.

Tiu^n, like many young women in nineteenth-century Taiwan, was raised outside of her birth family from a young age according to the practice of minor marriage. "As was the custom in Go Kho-khiⁿ", Tiuⁿ was transferred to another family, that of Tan Chiau (陳鳥) and Tiuⁿ Si (張氏), Tiun's *yangmu*, when she was three *sui* to be raised as a bride for their son (Zhang, 1987, 1). Minor marriages appear to have been more popular among Han families in Taiwan than in similar regions of China proper, and more popular in northern Taiwan where Tiuⁿ grew up than any other regions of Taiwan. In the second half of the nineteenth century, minor marriages made up as many as 48.5 per cent of all marriages in the region (Chuang and Wolf, 1995, 784–785). Marriage in Taiwan and throughout Qing China was formalized via marriage contracts between the husband and the parents of the bride, which established a bride-price to be paid to the birth family in return for their relinquishing all rights over the woman to her husband and his family. In late nineteenth-century Taiwan, the demand for brides significantly exceeded the supply, in part because of the gender imbalances caused by male immigration and female infanticide discussed above.

One way for a family to lessen the expense of acquiring a bride for their son and spread that expense out over time was to bring her into their household when she was very young and raise her alongside the boy whom she would one day marry. Since raising a child was both expensive and involved a high risk of loss given the number of girls who never grew up to be marriageable women, the bride-price for a child-bride was significantly less than that of a fifteen-year-old woman of marriageable age. The younger the girl at the time of purchase, the less expensive the bride's price. Minor marriages allowed local families to avoid having to compete with the increased demand for women caused by the large male immigrant population. In many cases families would search for a suitable bride for their sons while they were still infants, and the new child-bride could immediately start participating in the family economy by helping to care for her future husband. For the bride's birth family minor marriage also increased the likelihood that their daughter would remain part of a local household close to their own in an era when families' mobility was increasing dramatically. In this way, ironically, the decision to arrange a childhood marriage for a daughter was often born out of the desire to keep that daughter close to home.

As with infanticide, many scholars have attributed the practice of minor marriage to poverty. It has been argued that both the parents who sought to arrange marriages for their infant daughters and those who paid for these young girls to marry their sons chose these strategies due to a lack of resources. Chuang and Wolf contest both theses. "The evidence is unequivocal. Sopi Sa's comparison of three social strata in Taipei City shows that among men born in the years 1886–1905 the frequency of minor marriages was higher among shopkeepers, clerks, and minor government officials than among coolies, street vendors, and rickshawmen" (Chuang and Wolf, 1995, 788). Poverty does not correspond with higher rates of minor marriage. The social class most drawn to the economic advantages of minor marriage was the same class that was most likely to choose infanticide as a method to safeguard the socio-economic hierarchies within the family—the newly emerging middle class.

> The very high frequency of minor marriages in north-
> ern Taiwan was a direct result of an unbalanced sex ratio

and an affluent economy. Both, in turn, were consequences of the rapid and very successful development
of Taiwan's tea trade. The opportunities created by the
need for both skilled and unskilled labor in Taipei's tea
warehouses attracted large numbers of male immigrants from southern Taiwan and from established tea-
growing districts on the China mainland. Many were
assisted in this by foreign firms such as Dodd's and Tait's.
These men earned high wages and created in Taipei City
a demand for women that could not be satisfied by the
locally available supply.

(Chuang and Wolf, 1995, 791)

The increasing competition for wives in northern Taiwan probably
also contributed to the decreasing trend in excess female infant
mortality described by Olds. Even before Japanese rule opened
new economic opportunities for women to join the labor force,
the value of women as wives had risen well above the cost associated with raising them as daughters. In an atmosphere of such
high demand, who could afford to euthanize infant girls?

Adoptive families, on the other hand, were notorious for their
ill-treatment of their child-bride or *simpua* (童養媳). Adoptive
families were widely portrayed in both Chinese and Western literature as "indifferent or even abusive" (King, 2014, 32). At best,
adoptive parents "treated their young daughters-in-law no better than they treated domestic servants"; at worst, they were
held prisoner, like chattel slaves. Tiuⁿ's life as a *simpua* has generally been portrayed the same way. Tiuⁿ was continually diso-
bedient and was punished frequently and severely. She tried to
run away from her *yangmu* (adoptive mother) and return home

on multiple occasions. *Simpua* were allowed to visit their birth-parents each year during the New Year. During these visits, Tiuⁿ would find any excuse to delay her return, even throwing herself in the mud to ruin her holiday clothing (CPC Archives 2009-5004-2-26, 2–3). Once, according to her nephew, Tiuⁿ arrived at her birthparents' home in the middle of the night during a rainstorm, angry and hurt after a fight with her *yangmu* (adoptive mother) over a bag of peanuts. Her birthmother and grandmother both pleaded with her father to allow her to stay, but instead he carried her back to her *yangmu*'s home (Zhang, 1987, 1).

Tiuⁿ's relationship with her *yangmu* was greatly exacerbated by the death of her intended child-groom sometime "before Tiuⁿ turned twelve [*sui*]". Tiuⁿ's *yangmu* blamed her for having attracted the evil spirits that caused her son's death (Zhang, 1987, 1). None of the extant sources recount the cause of Tiuⁿ's intended's demise, nor even his name let alone his age when he died, so it is impossible to assess what actually killed him or the degree to which Tiuⁿ's care for her husband might have been viewed by her *yangmu* as a contributory factor in his death. As mentioned above, many child-brides were young girls whose first relationship with their infant husbands was similar to that of a babysitter or au pair, but there is no clear evidence that this was the case in Tiuⁿ's first marriage. The loss of a son was a significant blow to Tiuⁿ's *yangmu*'s status within her family. Perhaps the adoptive mother was no longer a favored wife of her own husband Tan Chiau, and without a son, had no secure means of supporting herself when her own son was gone. Tan Chiau died not long after this, an event that made Tiuⁿ's adoptive mother's situation even more desperate. Unable to own property or leave her home in search of outside employment, there were few prospects for a sonless widow to support herself in nineteenth-century Taiwan.

Tiuⁿ's first husband's death dashed Tiuⁿ's *yangmu*'s hopes of a comfortable future. At the same time, it also left Tiuⁿ Chhang-miâ in one of the most precarious social positions in Qing China— that of a *zhennü* (貞女), or virtuous maiden. Although Tiuⁿ was herself still a child when her child-husband died, she was also considered a widow under Qing law. Because she was childless, her status in the household of her would-have-been-husband was that of an unwanted servant—a status comparable to a chattel slave (Lu, 2009). One sensibility common in premodern Taiwan frowned upon widows remarrying, and it appears that Tiuⁿ's *yangmu* held to this line of thinking.

Tiuⁿ's adoptive mother insisted that the only "proper" thing for Tiuⁿ to do was to follow her husband by killing herself, and even attempted to help by restricting her access to adequate food and clothing. Although widow-suicide was outlawed by the Qing, it remained the second most common response of a *zhennü* (a maiden widow) to the death of their betrothed (Mann, 2007, 32–33). In Taiwan, because of the high demand for brides caused by the greatly skewed sex-ratio, there was still a fairly strong "second-hand market" for widows, so a *zhennü* could still command a reasonable bride-price—especially if she were attractive, chaste, and her feet were bound. But Tiuⁿ's adoptive mother's grief for her lost son must have outweighed her esti-mation of her *simpua*'s (adopted daughter-in-law) resale value. When Tiuⁿ Chhang-miâ failed to do the honorable thing and commit suicide and refused to waste away and die from hunger fast enough, her *yangmu* placed a blanket over Tiu^n's face and attempted to help her commit suicide.

Zhang Yuehan's account tells of a night when Tiu^n returned to the household of her birth family during a rainstorm, badly beaten during a physical altercation with her *yangmu*. According to this account, Tiu^n's *yangmu* also regularly engaged in other forms of neglect, such as only feeding Tiu^n potato peels and peanut shells. The night that Tiu^n returned to her birth home after her *yangmu* tried to kill her, her father refused to accept her back into his household despite the pleading of several of his relatives. Tiu^n was given some medicine but not even allowed to stay the night. Soon after this, Tiu^n went to live with her grandparents (her *yangmu*'s husband's parents), who would be responsible for raising her until she could be remarried or contracted as a bondservant with another household (Zhang, 1987, 2). The account in the Zhang family genealogy does not include the same details of neglect and abuse that Zhang Yuehan's does but does claim that her *yangfu* (her adoptive father) ordered that her feet be bound, "to make three-inch lotuses" when she was ten (after her intended had died) (Zhang, 2006, 26). This process, which usually began much earlier, would almost certainly have felt like daily physical abuse to a young adolescent woman.

Greenhaulgh suggested that rather than infanticide and widow suicide, the primary cause of excess female mortality in Taiwan was the prevalence of foot-binding (Greenhaulgh, 1977, 1). Dr David Ko vigorously contests her thesis that infections caused by bones accidentally broken and wounded feet bound with rags soaked in septic animal blood were a significant cause of death for young girls.

The owner of one of the world's largest collections of foot-binding artifacts, and himself a podiatric surgeon, Ko has written several books in Taiwan on the history, methodology, and aesthetics of the practice. He claims that the slow-rearticulation of ligaments caused by the foot-binding process did not result in broken bones or even permanent structural changes to women's feet. Nevertheless, foot-binding was one example of how social hierarchies were etched onto the bodies of Taiwanese women. It caused significant pain, both for the young girls who underwent the process and the older women who later reversed it by liberating their feet; it was certainly one of the perils of growing up as a girl in Taiwan.

Foot-binding was vilified by Western missionary observers, who characterized it not only as abusive to women, but indicative of a deviant and sinful sexuality. Unsurprisingly, there seems to have been some effort in Presbyterian sources to conceal the fact that Tiuⁿ's feet had once been bound. Missionaries saw the custom of foot-binding as proof of the moral decrepitude of imperial China. Not only did it represent the pinnacle of patriarchal dominance discussed by Dorothy Ko, but imprinted this dominance upon the female body in a manner that was easily characterized as physical abuse. At the same time, foot-binding was steeped in culture or sensuality which, to the Victorian mind, was the epitome of lewdness. Even before Rev. MacGowen founded the Natural Foot Society in 1875, the eradication of this custom was one of the primary goals of the Protestant Missionary movement in China (Ko, 2008, 219). Foot-binding was so frowned upon that when George Leslie Mackay decided to seek a Taiwanese woman to marry, one of his only criteria for a prospective bride was that she not have bound feet. (Mackay also indicated that he would like a wife who was in good health, had an upright appearance (容貌端正), and was not too unattractive.) While Giam Cheng-hoa advised Mackay that although there were many young women around who were both healthy and upright, finding one whose feet were not bound would be difficult. This requirement, more than any other, was said to have led George Leslie Mackay to choose to marry Tiuⁿ, as she was the only woman to be found whose feet were unbound (Tan Heng-teng Sao, 1992, 194). Tiuⁿ's unbound feet were, for the rest of her life, promoted as the primary feature that enabled her to obtain her advantageous marriage. It was so important that when she passed away special efforts were made at her funeral to continue to conceal the fact that her feet had once been bound.

The practice of foot-binding has roots in Chinese civilization as far back as the Song Dynasty or even earlier, but was not widely practiced until the latter part of the Qing Dynasty. Sometime in the late seventeenth or early eighteenth century, foot-binding became associated with Han cultural elitism, and became an important status symbol differentiating women of upper-class Han families from their Manchu counterparts, considered by some to be less culturally refined. It had become widespread enough that the Qing passed a law against foot-binding in 1847 (Saman, 2014, 4), but the Qing attempts to suppress the practice only seem to have encouraged its spread. By the nineteenth century nearly 40 per cent of ethnic Han women had bound feet (Ko, 2008, 4–7). Many scholars believe that the high social value placed on bound feet during this era diffused downward from the gentry to the middle classes as part of a process of Veblenian "conspicuous consumption" (Saman, 2014, 2).

Many second-wave feminist scholars from the 1960s and 1970s have held that foot-binding was an overt attempt to control female productive and reproductive labor by dramatically limiting the physical mobility of upper-middle-class women (Greenhaulgh, 1977). (The first wave of course was the nineteenth-century feminists, whereas today many women are characterizing a third wave of feminism focusing on universal self-determination and genderless rights.) Among the advocates of this "labor-control" interpretation of foot-binding, Bossen and Gates make a particularly strong argument for the association of bound feet with handicraft work (particularly weaving) done by women and young girls while sitting in the home. Comparing data from across more than a dozen counties in China, they found "that mothers and older women bound the feet of the girls in their households to assert control over their labor and then shifted the blame for its bodily costs from the mother they lived with to an unknown mother-in-law who would treat them badly if they did not have bound feet and could not work with their hands." Girls who were occupied in hand-labor in the home, whether it be in the production of textiles, hats, nets or some other commodity, were 2.144 times more likely to be foot-bound than girls who were not so occupied. (Bosson and Gates, 2017, 10). Of course, it is difficult to be certain whether handiwork led to increased levels of foot-binding or whether foot-bound girls were more often employed in sedentary handiwork because that is what they could do.

Unfortunately, less research has been done concerning the economic activities performed by women whose feet were not bound during this era, so there is little consensus concerning the economic value gained from binding a girl's feet. Some scholars counter that girls' feet were not bound to compel them to engage in particular types of labor, but rather to prevent them from being compelled to other (less desirable) labor such as fieldwork. A woman who had bound feet did not need to work to support herself—in fact she was wealthy enough that she did not even have to walk.

Other scholars suggest that foot-binding was primarily a delicate and erotic aesthetic, which had little to do with political or economic control of women (Ko, 2008). There is an extensive literature from this period extolling the three-inch lotus foot as the iconic symbol of female sensuality. The connotation of carnal pleasures which Western missionaries used to demonize foot-binding unsurprisingly magnified its allure. Most accounts of the origins of foot-binding trace it back to the enticing movements of imperial dancers balancing on their lotus feet. Still, it is difficult to determine whether late Qing Dynasty foot-binding grew in popularity because of the erotic literature, or whether the unprecedented growth of foot-binding during this period gave rise to this literary genre.

Most girls who underwent the procedure began binding their feet around the age of five. Literate women referred to the beginning of foot-binding as "losing their milk-teeth", because most girls lost their baby teeth around the same time their feet were first bound (Mann, 2007, 25–27). It was done by carefully rolling the smaller toes under the foot and tying them tightly into place with a silk cravat. The cravat was then used to draw the toes in close to the heel, heightening the arch and shortening the length of the foot overall. Contrary to a widely held misperception, bones were not broken during this process. The ligaments and other soft tissues that connect the bones were gradually trained to assume a permanent deformity, while the continued growth of the feet was inhibited. In order to achieve the ideal "three-inch lotus" feet, foot-binding had to begin early, before bones and ligaments were fully developed, but not before the child had learned to walk well enough to maintain her balance on her thus misshapen and tender feet.

It has been difficult for scholars to explain the particular prevalence of foot-binding in Taiwan. In mainland China, as discussed above, foot-binding is most highly correlated with women's role in weaving silk and other textiles: work which required long hours of sitting inside the home. Weaving, however, was not a significant factor in most Taiwanese household economies. Furthermore, if Olds is correct in his assertion that the Japanese prohibition of foot-binding led directly to an increase in the economic value of women's labor, then it follows that foot-binding was highly popular in Taiwan despite the fact that it did limit women's economic value (Olds, 2006, 215).

According to Melissa Brown, most young girls engaged in foot-binding because they believed it would help them secure a more advantageous marriage. In her field interviews, most of the women who chose to bind their daughters' feet, and nearly all of the girls who chose to bind their own feet, cited marriage prospects as their primary motive. Brown also claims that foot-binding served as a symbol of status that reinforced political and social hierarchies between women within households, but that economic considerations were secondary at best (Brown, 2016, 503–504).

Although Brown's research shows that foot-binding did not tend to result in more advantageous marriages for its practitioners in mainland China, the *belief* that it *could* was nevertheless a significant factor in the decision to bind girls' feet. In northern Taiwan where the scarcity of brides caused by high infant mortality rates and excess male in- migration had already inflated the marriage market, foot-binding may have been seen as a way to increase a family's ability to capitalize on what was perceived as girls' most important economic contribution (Brown, 2016, 515). This added to the fact that foot-binding was widely held as a form of cultural resistance against the Manchu rulers of the Qing Dynasty (Ko, 2008, 132–133). It may have made bound feet particularly attractive in Taiwan. In Taiwan, where resistance to Qing authority was a long-held tradition, foot-binding as a southern-Han status marker may have represented a larger than average premium.

The Hokkien segment of the Taiwanese Han population are believed to have had the highest proportion of foot-bound women in the Qing Empire, and the Japanese Census of 1905 indicates that more than 90 per cent of Han women born in Taiwan before 1895 had bound feet, but this number (more than twice Ko's estimate for mainland China) is likely exaggerated. Since Hakka women did not bind their feet and Hakka constituted a significant Han ethnic minority in nineteenth-century Taiwan, in order for foot-binding to reach 90 per cent, virtually 100 per cent of all Hokkien women would have had to have had bound feet. Most scholars doubt this level of ubiquity and suggest that the exaggerated level of foot-binding reported was due to the prejudice (and perhaps the laxity) of Japanese census takers, who assumed bound feet for all Fujian women, verified or not. But records do indicate that census takers did actually examine the feet of many women. Tiuⁿ, herself, was never personally interviewed by census takers. Her name was listed in the 1915 census, but the status of her feet is left blank—neither listed as bound or unbound—which suggests that at least in her particular case the census takers did not make any assumptions they could not corroborate.

Throughout his lifetime, George Leslie Mackay maintained that he specifically chose Tiuⁿ to be his wife because she did not have bound feet and all of the Canadian sources about Tiuⁿ's life claim that her feet were not bound, even as some seemed to doubt the veracity of their claim. Mary Junor's letter to the Presbyterian Record in November of 1879 that explained that Tiuⁿ could wear foreign shoes because her feet "were never very much nor very long bound" is the only hint in anglophone sources that anyone from Canada ever knew Tiuⁿ's feet had been bound (Junor, 1879, 301).

Tiuⁿ's adoptive grandmother's statement in response to George Leslie Mackay's three criteria, that "perhaps Tiuⁿ did not wish to bind her feet", has been interpreted by many to mean that up until that point (when Tiuⁿ was fifteen or sixteen *sui*) her feet had been bound. Chen Meiliao once claimed that there is no proof that Tiuⁿ's feet were ever "unbound", by which she meant to imply that Tiuⁿ may have continued to bind her feet throughout her lifetime (Chen, 2001, 96), to which Louise Gamble replied that there was also no (authoritative) evidence that her feet were ever bound at all (Gamble, 2018, 1).

Chen's claim appears to have been based on the fact that Tiuⁿ was not listed as *jiejiao* (解腳) or having "liberated" feet, and in the absence of *jiejiao* a Fujian woman would have been presumed to have had bound feet (especially if it could be demonstrated that her feet were at some point bound). But the Japanese census takers never directly inspected Tiu^n's feet. Although the Japanese completed three household reviews during Tiu^n's lifetime (1905, 1915, and 1925), Tiu^n (like her son) carefully avoided each of these censuses. Her name appears in the 1915 census as the mother of her younger daughter, Elizabeth Mackay (Xie Yili, 偕以利), but she was never directly interviewed. For this reason, some scholars believe this column in the census was left blank because no one ever confirmed whether her feet were bound or not. Nor are there any medical records remaining from Tiu^n's life to confirm or deny the condition of her feet. The narrative in the Zhang family genealogy published more than fifty years after Tiu^n's death remains the only source that expressly attests that her feet were ever bound. For this reason, widely divergent narratives concerning Tiu^n's personal experience with foot-binding and the impact of that experience upon her life's work continue to persist.

Infanticide, namelessness, minor marriage, and foot-binding are perhaps the most notorious examples of the dangers of being born a woman in late imperial Taiwan, and Tiu^n Chhang-miâ's life was certainly affected by all of them. Although Tiu^n's personal experience with these trials may have been exaggerated by orientalist writers attempting to demonize Confucian patriarchal systems and mobilize sentiment to change them, these dangers were no less real. What we do know of Tiu^n's childhood does speak to the humbleness and precarity of her origins. By the age of ten, Tiu^n had been purchased, married, widowed, discarded, and abandoned. Her dead husband's grandparents had saved her life and taken her in in the hopes that someday they might be able to recover the bride-price paid for her, but to do this they had to start binding her feet—a process that should have been started half a decade earlier. She had tried to run away several times but was always returned. There was nowhere for her to go. In all of the subsequent versions of her narrative these early childhood hardships serve as both the basis and proof of Tiuⁿ's strength and grace.

3
From "Little Onion" to "Brilliant One"

Becoming the woman who made Mackay a superstar

While women's lives in premodern Taiwan certainly had their challenges, Laurel Bossen and Hill Gates point out that the narrative of female victimhood can be problematic as well.

> Whether the oppressive forces were defined as patriarchy, feudalism, capitalism, or all three, the prevailing view in the West and among Chinese reformers was that in traditional patriarchal society, Chinese women had miserable lives. In the 1990s, attention to new sources written by or about women sought to rescue women from the image of unremitting victimhood by drawing on new literary sources to show that women found ways to express "agency" despite their many social and economic constraints.
>
> (Bossen and Gates, 2017, 13)

In other words, women were not merely the passive victims of "Confucian" society, they were active participants who helped to construct and define it. Describing women as helpless objects of society obscures everything they did.

One variant of the victim narrative that Meiliao Chen calls "the Cinderella story", in which a young girl is elevated from a humble status to become an influential woman because of her romance and marriage to a wealthy and important man, is just as dismissive of women's autonomy as the orientalist critique is. Tiuⁿ Chhang-miâ has often been described as a Cinderella-like heroine because of her marriage to an eminent foreigner, Dr George Leslie Mackay.

Credited with building sixty mission stations, a hospital, a college, and a school for girls, and baptizing more than 3,000 Taiwanese converts, Mackay is often heralded as the most successful Protestant missionary of all time (Ion, 2005, 186). Tiuⁿ's fame certainly has much to do with her husband's success. Her studies, her travels, her fundraising, and her leadership in education and in the Presbyterian Church of Taiwan were all made possible by her marriage to the Canadian missionary. But Tiuⁿ met and married Mackay *before* he built the missions or the hospital or the schools that made them famous, and *they* built them *together*. It seems that Mackay could not have built the mission he did without Tiuⁿ and especially without the support of her family. More than a third of the missions that Mackay founded and the native preachers who administered them were the fruit of the Tan clan's efforts, the very clan Tiuⁿ came from. Another third arose from the families of their closest commercial and political alliances. While Mackay often cited the novelty of his marriage to a local woman as drawing large crowds to his mission (in particular women), the political and economic benefits of being associated with what became known as the "Tan family business" had a similar effect. Tiuⁿ was not merely the "great woman behind the great man". She and her family turned the man she married into the "great man" he became by building the mission that was his legacy. All this came to Mackay by virtue of his advantageous marriage to Tiuⁿ. If anything, George Leslie Mackay, the husband, was the "Cinderella" in their story, rather than the other way round.

George Leslie Mackay arrived in Taiwan in 1872, following a wave of Protestant missionaries that had been called to mainland China since the 1860s by the example of William Chalmer Burns and Hudson Taylor and their China Inland Mission. Thousands of European and North American Protestants responded to the call to introduce the Bible to the world's largest empire in the second half of the nineteenth century, and unlike anywhere else in the world, diverse sects of Protestants cooperatively planned their mission activities so as not to end up in direct competition with each other. Mackay had met Burns when he was very young and grew up hoping to follow in his footsteps. He attended the seminaries at Princeton and Edinburgh and was sponsored by the Canada Presbyterian Church as their first foreign missionary to China. When he met with representatives of the English Presbyterian Church in Fujian at Amoy (Xiamen), he chose northern Taiwan as his mission field because no other missionary had claimed it before. He knew nothing of Taiwan or its people, not even the language.

Mackay rented an unused carriage-house and spent the first few weeks of his mission trading candies and trinkets to the young boys who tended water-buffalo on the Tamkang river in return for language lessons. He had a servant, whom the English missionaries, stationing in southern Taiwan, had assigned to look after Mackay. But this servant soon left. Mackay claimed the servant left out of frustration with Mackay's incessant questions, but it seems to be the arrival of a new tutor that caused the servant's departure (Mackay, 1900, 196). On April 19, 1872, just nine days after Mackay had rented the carriage-house, a young man, Giam Chheng-hoa, presented himself and offered to become Mackay's "first student".

Giam was well-educated by then Taiwanese standards. The only son of a widow, Giam had been raised by a priest at the Tan family temple where he learned to read and write Mandarin well. While he spoke the same Fujian dialect that was prevalent throughout Taiwan, he had travelled as far as Beijing as the personal attendant to a Taiwanese tea merchant and was familiar with the Mandarin dialect used by Qing officials. He spent three days at Mackay's apartment, looking over Mackay's language books and the copies of Bible translations that Mackay had received from the English Mission and trying to discuss these with Mackay, before he agreed to work with him. Mackay offered Giam a job as his house-servant, and proclaimed him to be his "first student", but in fact Giam became Mackay's Chinese teacher.

Within a month, Giam had invited his mother's mother-in-law, Tan Thah-so, to come downriver from Go Kho-khiⁿ to listen to Mackay preach. She in turn invited Mackay to come preach at her brother-in-law's village. Mackay made no note of the people who travelled with Tan Thah-so at the time; in fact he did not even note it in his diary. It was not until 1895 when his memoirs were released that he recounted this important meeting with Tan Thah-so, his "first female convert". Tan Thah-so had already assumed guardianship over Tiuⁿ after the attempted smother, so it is possible that Tiuⁿ was there with her grandmother too, and that this was the first time she saw Mackay. Three months later, Mackay accepted their invitation to preach at Go Kho-khiⁿ for the first time. Tan Pao, Tiuⁿ's uncle and the headman of the village, hung a scroll with the ten commandments written in Mandarin in front of his home and gave Mackay an abandoned granary to repurpose it into northern Taiwan's first mission station. Although Mackay would not have noticed a young girl of ten or twelve at the time, Tiuⁿ was already there living in the home of Tan Pao's sister-in-law, and certainly would have seen Mackay. Even then, her family was already planning the spread of the Presbyterian mission and engineering Mackay's future success.

The next spring, Giam "graduated" and was certified by Mackay as being ready to preach on his own. Mackay had acquired several new students who continued to assist him as he travelled around northern Taiwan preaching and offering free medicine in search of converts. So Giam took over the mission station at Go Kho-khiⁿ and became northern Taiwan's first native preacher. Tan Thah-so and her daughter-in-law's *simpua* (child-bride), Tiuⁿ Chhang-miâ, became his first two students, and Giam's path from student to teacher with his own mission station became the blueprint for Mackay's mission expansion.

Each year new students—mostly from the Tan clan, but also from the wealthy Li and Lim families around Go Kho-khiⁿ—moved to Tamsui to study with Mackay. They did not stay in Tamsui, but itinerated around the countryside. Throughout the first five years of his mission, Mackay spent nearly as many days travelling as he did at home in Tamsui. He and his students walked around northern Taiwan, from village to village, offering medicine, songs, and Christian teaching. While Mackay taught his students to become Christian lay-preachers, they were teaching him the language and geography of Taiwan. Because not every community was equally safe, Mackay's students carefully chose the places they travelled. Mackay's early students frequently introduced him to villages where their kinship networks were the strongest. After a year or two of study, each student would graduate and choose a village in which to build his own mission station, where he would live and teach.

These native preachers frequently chose sites that were either near their family homes, or close to their important business partners. In this way the Go Kho-khiⁿ community greatly influenced the geospatial expansion of the early mission. The Canada Presbyterian Mission's growth followed the kinship and business networks of the Tan, Lim, and Li families very closely. At the same time, the emerging British mercantile networks supporting the tea and camphor trades closely followed the Canadian Mission, which trained many middle-class workers to read and write the Anglicized version of Chinese known as POJ in which they conducted business (Dodge, 2021, 194–195). The extraterritorial rights afforded to missionaries and their "helpers" pursuant to the Peking convention of 1860 and the Treaty of Nanking also provided extensive legal protection for people and businesses working for the Presbyterian mission within these emerging networks.

While the British never attempted to colonize Taiwan in the way that they had seized political and economic control over so many other territories in locations from Africa to India and the Americas, they nevertheless exerted a constant threat of military intervention that ensured that both local leaders and the Qing Empire would accommodate their demands to avoid a more complete occupation. In 1868, the British navy deployed battleships to Taiwan twice to ensure the privileged status of their citizens was honored there. When a Presbyterian missionary from the English Presbyterian Church was accused of poisoning a local girl and beaten by a crowd, three British warships bombarded Takao until the mission's demand for ten thousand silver dollars in compensation was met. Thirty Taiwanese died and many buildings were destroyed in the assault. A month later, when an agent of a British tea merchant was assaulted outside of Bang-kah in present-day Taipei, the HMS Algerine merely had to sail into the mouth of the Tamkang river for the local Tao-tai (道臺 or magistrate) to offer a $4,800 reparation payment (Tsai, 2014, 83).

After 1868, the British Consulate at Tamsui was recognized as the primary point of contact between the Qing administration and all other foreign powers operating in Taiwan. Japan would launch a brief punitive campaign into southern Taiwan in 1874 in response to the capture and execution of fifty-four Ryukyuan fishermen that ran aground there three years earlier, but the expedition was defeated by malaria and dysentery (Katz, 1996). France also attempted an invasion in 1884 with similar results, but the British remained neutral (and even supported the Qing) in each of these campaigns and did not use military force to assert their prerogatives on the island again after 1868.

The year after the Japanese incursion into southern Taiwan, a second Canadian missionary, Dr J. B. Fraser, arrived in Tamsui with his family to help administer the rapidly growing Canada

Presbyterian mission, but he did not last long. Mrs Fraser died of infection four days after giving birth to their fourth child in October 1877. Dr Fraser left for Canada with their children a week later (Mackay's diaries, October 2–10, 1877). This was a double loss for the mission. Not only had it lost its medical doctor—one of the most important services Taiwanese natives looked for at the mission—but it had lost its only female missionary.

Nanwainūnei, the belief mentioned in the previous chapter that women should control the sphere inside the home while men handled the outer sphere, made it socially inappropriate for a man to hold conversations with women outside his own family, and especially outside of the home. This was considered a tremendous obstacle for male missionaries in East Asia, as it was nearly impossible for them to proselytize women and children who spent most of their time sequestered inside family compounds. Tan Thah-so, Mackay's first female convert, may have felt protected to some degree from ostracization by her status as the widow of the village headman's older brother as well as the entourage that travelled with her, but most women were not willing to be seen attending Mackay's sermons in public. Nor was Mackay (or his young male students) apt to be invited into their homes to speak with women there.

In Canada (and throughout the Protestant West), at the same time, women were increasingly seen as the key to the successful spread of Christianity. The ideal of Christian womanhood common in Canada held that women (although still imagined as intellectually inferior to men) had a special, "simplistic", and purer form of faith that was both stronger and closer to God (Welter, 1966). This deep womanly faith was considered vital to the spread of Christianity to future generations. Mackay's supporters in Canada had long been pressuring him to marry and take on a helpmeet to help draw more women to the mission, but Mackay had resisted their pressure. Perhaps he hoped Mrs Fraser might fill this need, or perhaps he was just young and shy, but either way Mackay refused to entertain discussions of marrying a Canadian to help him in his missionary work. Mrs Fraser's untimely death rekindled the urgency for a feminine worker in the mission, but it also strengthened Mackay's belief that Canadian women were not hardy enough to survive Taiwan's harsh environment. If he was to submit to the pressure to choose a wife, he was determined not to choose one from Canada.

Just weeks after Dr Fraser's departure with five children and an unnamed wetnurse to return to Canada, Mackay announced his intention to take a local bride. He explained in a letter to Professor McLaren of the Foreign Mission Committee (FMC) that he felt that marrying a Taiwanese woman was the only way that he would be able to draw Taiwanese women to the church.

> I have for a long time been grieved at heart to see the women here despised, forgotten and left within the home, whilst husbands and bros &c. attended service… Such being the case, after long and prayerful consideration for guidance I have determined (D. V.) to take a Chinese lady to become my helpmeet and labor for these perishing thousands.
>
> (Gamble and Chen, 2015, 175)

Although there were several attempts by his superiors in Canada to change his mind, Mackay had already entered a marriage contract with Tiuⁿ's parents by the time he had written to them. According to Tan Hun-teng So (陳雲騰嫂), the marriage arrangements were made six months before the May 1878 wedding, meaning that Mackay had committed to his future bride at least a month before writing to the FMC. (Tan Heng-teng so, 194). Tan Hun-teng was the youngest son of Tan Pao, the headman of Go Kho-khiⁿ, a cousin of Tiuⁿ Chhang-miâ and one of Mackay's students. He later married Giam Yu-Niang (嚴玉娘), Giam Cheng-hoa's younger sister, who is said to be the original source of the story.

Giam had tried for more than a year to convince Mackay to take a Taiwanese bride, but the idea was nothing new. The Dutch Reformed minister Candidius had suggested intermarriage between Dutch men and Taiwanese women as a method to speed up the Christianization of the island as early as the seventeenth century (Chiu, 2008, 145–146). The belief that male missionaries had little hope of proselytizing women and children within the context of East Asian societies was also widespread long before Mackay arrived. Much like the details of Tiuⁿ's childhood, the reasons why Mackay should seek to marry a native woman were established long before he and she ever met. Mackay eventually agreed to take a Taiwanese wife, but on some conditions. He would only accept a girl who was "healthy, of upright appearance and didn't have bound feet" (Tan Heng-teng so, 194). Much of Tiuⁿ's subsequent life would be narrated so as to conform with these criteria, considered essential for the wife of an upright Protestant minister.

While healthy upright women were plentiful, an "upright" woman whose feet weren't bound was hard to find. Even though

Taiwanese indigenous women and Hakkas (between them nearly a quarter of the population of Taiwan) did not practice foot-binding, nearly all of the "upright" "aristocratic" women of Fujian descent did. Thah-so suggested that her granddaughter, Tiu^n, "perhaps did not want to bind her feet" (Lee, 2014, 38), and so Tiu^n was presented as the only woman in northern Taiwan who met all three of Mackay's criteria. Mackay asked Giam to arrange an opportunity to look at her before consenting, so the two of them visited the Tan tea plantation in Go Kho-khi^n to spy on her while she fed the ducks. Mackay remained skeptical, so Thah-So proposed that Tiu^n spend six months indoors doing only light chores to lighten her complexion and "pretty her up" (Tan Heng-teng so, 194).

Around this time Mackay was also worried that there were not enough students enrolled at many of the mission stations. Giam suggested that the mission might attract more students if he offered a prize of some sort. Mackay promptly posted a Bible-reading competition offering one Mexican silver dollar each for the best boy and best girl reader of POJ. Within a month, enrolment at the Go Kho-khi^n mission station had climbed to over one hundred students, and at the end of the month, Tiu^n Chhang-miâ won the girls' prize (Tang, 2001). The competition so pleased Mackay that he continued the custom throughout his mission, offering annual examinations with cash prizes open to all the students and native preachers in the mission. Tiu^n's ability to earn money via her studies also changed her status at home. After she won her first prize, she was allowed back into her *yangmu*'s home, where she was relieved of her farm labor duties. Tiu^n's ability to earn a few dollars each month reading and teaching the

Bible, at last, convinced her adoptive mother that she had some value. By the time she was seventeen *sui* (probably sixteen years old), Tiuⁿ was teaching other women to read and write POJ, and routinely earned a dollar a month for her efforts (Forsberg, 2012, 113–114).

Although Tiuⁿ seems to have been the only potential bride in northern Taiwan that suited Mackay's criteria and whose family was not averse to marrying their daughter to a foreigner, Mackay was still hesitant. Tiuⁿ's studiousness, however, appears to have changed his mind. When pressed by his students as to whether he had chosen a bride, Mackay replied, "Chhang-a, because she truly is *Chhang-mi*â (聰明 or brilliant)" (Zhang, 1987, 3). Tan Heng-Teng acted as the marriage broker. Tiuⁿ's *yangmu* agreed to the marriage in exchange for thirty silver dollars and an allowance of three dollars a month until she was a hundred years old. Mackay agreed. In December, he wrote to his superiors of his intent to marry a local girl and in February Mackay baptized Chhang-a, officially naming her Tiuⁿ Chhang-miâ (張聰明)—a homophone of her familiar name that emphasized her brilliance rather than her acerbity. Mackay's baptismal record is the earliest document that names Tiuⁿ. It lists her as being eighteen sui in February of 1878, and is the only original record of Tiuⁿ's age. They were married on May 27, 1878. Tiuⁿ was no longer referred to as Min either. Instead, Mackay nicknamed her Minnie, in deference to the Roman goddess of wisdom, Minerva—the nickname by which she is most remembered in English (Gamble and Chen, 2012, I, 1, 175).

Despite the fact that Mackay was an ordained minister, his wedding to Tiuⁿ was conducted according to Chinese tradition and sanctified by a secular service performed by the British Consul, rather than a religious service within the church. Another ordained Canada Presbyterian missionary, Kenneth Junor, arrived with his family just two weeks after the wedding to assist with the mission at Tamsui, but rather than waiting to have a Christian ceremony conducted by a Presbyterian minister, Tiu^n and Mackay held their wedding while the Junors were still in transit (Mackay, diaries, May 27, 1878–June 12, 1878). A set of marriage contracts similar to those common in Taiwan at the time were signed. Tiu^n's adoptive mother executed a contract granting her permission to marry Mackay, but Mackay apparently doubted that her authority to grant Tiu^n's hand in marriage would be recognized in Canada and requested a second contract signed by Tiu^n's birthparents (Forsberg, 2012, 114).

Tiu^n, so the story goes, was indignant that her life should be determined either by the woman who tried to smother her or the man who sent her back to her after she did, and wrote her own statement declaring her love for Mackay and granting *herself* permission to marry the missionary. This token of consent, non-binding though it was, speaks to a new conception of feminist modernity that emerged specifically in Taiwanese space as the result of the confluence of contradictory traditions. The cultural imperative under which Mackay was operating directly contradicted the one in which Tiu^n lived.

Because Mackay could not accept Tiu^n's adopted mother's authority, but Taiwanese law did not validate that of her birth-father's, there was no one who clearly had the authority to approve Tiu^n's marriage to Mackay. Perhaps Tiu^n and Mackay agreed in that moment only a clear expression of her own consent would stand up to future criticisms, or maybe the British consul Alexander Frater felt compelled by the legal gray area their union created to demand a separate letter asserting Tiuⁿ's own consent to validate his own breach of tradition in endorsing their interracial union. Either way, Tiuⁿ's letter represents the oldest known example of a Taiwanese woman contracting her own marriage.

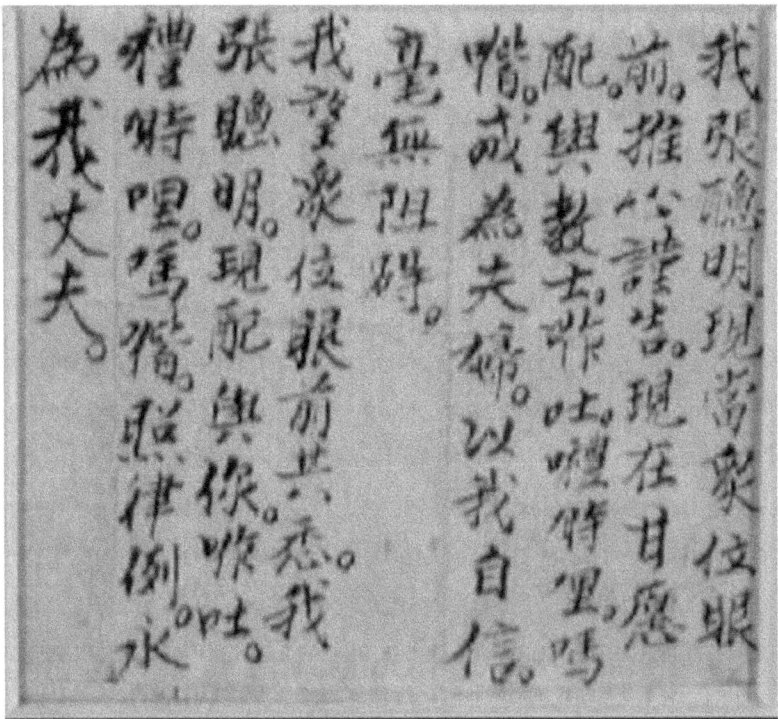

Figure 1 Tiuⁿ Chhang-miâ's self-written marriage contract reads: "I Tiuⁿ Chhang-miâ in the presence of all, solemnly announce that I marry Reverend Mackay willingly to be united as a married couple. This is done of my own free will, unhindered in any way. I wish you all now to bear witness that I, Tiuⁿ Chhang-miâ marry Reverend Mackay under the law for him to be my husband forever. (Courtesy of Aletheia University Archives—photograph of original displayed at the Mackay Museum Tamsui)

Although there were some abnormalities in the marriage contracts (most notably the omission of the bride-price Mackay paid for Tiuⁿ), the process of their marriage followed very closely to the traditional Taiwanese custom as described by David Jordan (Jordan, 1997). Mackay had given a gift to Tiuⁿ's parents when he had awarded Tiuⁿ the special three-dollar prize for her oration, which correlates with the first step of marriage *nacai* (納彩)—submitting a betrothal gift. He had formally asked for her name, the second step *wenming* (問名) when he baptized her. Tiuⁿ Si had accepted the thirty-dollar bride-price offered by the marriage broker Tan Heng-teng, fulfilling *nazheng* (納征), although there is no record of any gifts given to Mackay in return. *Qingqi* (請期—picking the date) and *qinying* (親迎—welcoming the bride to her new home) were both carried out in the process of choosing May 27 to bring Tiuⁿ to the consulate in Tamsui for the final ceremony.

Whether by Mackay's design or on the insistence of the Tan family who controlled Tiuⁿ's fate, or because of the uncertain legal authority of the British Consul, the first interracial union between British and Qing subjects was carefully orchestrated to meet all the traditional obligations of Chinese marriage as set out in the classic book of Rites except for *naji* (納吉), the customary divination request made by the groom's parents to determine the couple's compatibility, at the same time that it fulfilled all of the legal requirements for a British marriage as well. It is highly unlikely that Mackay's parents would have agreed to, let alone order, what they considered to be heathen astrological divinations as it would have been a clear violation of their Presbyterian faith. If Mackay's students who were negotiating the terms of the wedding contract had astrological charts drawn up on his behalf, it is similarly unlikely that Mackay would have acknowledged or kept them. Ultimately the marriage was deemed acceptable by the Taiwanese. Mackay unofficially became Taiwan's *nüxu* (女婿), or son-in-law.

Tiuⁿ was the first Taiwanese woman (and the first Qing Empire subject) to legally marry a Western missionary, and perhaps the first to legally marry any Westerner at all. Although there were numerous foreign men in Taiwan and throughout the Qing Empire that kept Chinese consorts, these women could only claim the status of unwed concubine at best. Mackay, of course, as a Presbyterian minister could not permit himself to engage in a relationship with a woman outside of formal marriage. His faith required that Mackay commit to Tiuⁿ as an equal partner in a way that no other Western man thitherto had. Subsequently, there were only two other such interracial marriages among missionaries and Chinese subjects in the nineteenth century, each of which resulted in punishment and censure. When George Parker of the China Inland Mission (CIM) married "Minnie" Parker in Tianshui in 1881, Hudson Taylor attempted to force him to resign from the ministry. This nearly ended in a schism when more than a dozen missionaries threatened to resign in support of Parker if Taylor Hudson did not personally approve the marriage. Seventeen years later, Anna Jakobsen's 1898 marriage to Cheng Hsiu-chi did not receive the same popular support from her colleagues. She was forced to leave the CIM and founded her own mission society (Austyn, 2007, 238–239). After that, interracial miscegenation between Protestant missionaries and Chinese subjects remained taboo until the second half of the twentieth century. There were similar attempts to dissuade Mackay from his decision to marry Tiu^n, but they opted to marry two weeks before anyone from the Canada Presbyterian Church was in Taiwan to object, and were already blessed with one healthy daughter and a second on the way before they arrived in Canada where the FMC could take up the question of whether or not to approve their union. There is no way of knowing whether or not Junor would have agreed to performing the marriage had they waited two weeks longer for his arrival, but clearly there was enough reason to doubt his support that Tiu^n and Mackay opted not to wait.

4
The native mission's gynocentric imaginary

Narratives are important. People compose stories to help them remember the important events and people of the past, but they also imprint cultural values upon those events within the structure of the narratives they construct. Anthropologists call the belief systems based on such narratives imaginaries. Imaginaries dramatically influence how people interact with the world around them: people act within the world according to what they believe about it. Imaginaries, as the term implies, are imagined and do not necessarily have to be "true" to influence the societies that believe in them. Myths, legends, and even unfounded biases and prejudices can have as substantial an influence on social construction as documented facts. This seems to be the case with Tiuⁿ and Mackay.

Tiuⁿ and Mackay knew that their marriage was unprecedented and very likely to set the tone for Anglo-Chinese relations for years to come. While Tiuⁿ was still a very young woman, largely motivated by a desire to escape her abusive childhood, Mackay was a thirty-four-year-old world-traveler who had studied theology and public speaking at Knox College in Toronto, Princeton in America, and Edinburgh in Scotland. When he carefully chose to plant the Canada Presbyterian Mission in northern Taiwan where no foreign missionary had operated before him in the hope of creating a community that was untainted by others, it was clear that he hoped his work would have historic significance. Similarly, when he chose to violate cultural taboos and marry across racial lines despite his brother's insistence that this was a horrible mistake, it seems certain that Mackay already had some conception of the values he hoped that his actions would come to represent. Most historians and anthropologists would agree that societies construct their histories and imbue them with meaning described above. The imaginaries in which Mackay and Tiuⁿ believed in turn influenced the way in which historical events were later woven into their community's self-identity.

In particular, the narratives on Tiuⁿ Chhang-miâ's work in the Presbyterian Church have been driven by a powerful imaginary that deemed Tiuⁿ's ability as an ethnic Chinese woman to draw other "native" women to the mission as the fundamental cause of the mission's unparalleled success. Although this imaginary was based upon mistaken or unproven claims, many people in Canada and Taiwan at the time believed it so that it became a Pentecostal force driving the growth of Presbyterianism in Taiwan.

Tiuⁿ's work was clearly one of the most important elements in the Canada Presbyterian Mission's success—not because she drew an unprecedented number of women to the mission, but because she and her husband were able to convince so many people that she did. Mackay himself became so firmly committed to this belief, and the theories he constructed to explain it, that he developed an entire missiological system organized around the native-woman myth that guided his work and the work of missionaries for generations to come.

According to Mackay's letters, he made the controversial decision to marry Tiu^n because he believed it was the best way he could benefit the mission (Forsberg, 2009). Her presence at public services as his wife would, in theory, enable other ethnic Chinese women to attend such services without incurring accusations of impropriety, and her ability to enter the homes of Chinese women and speak directly to them and their families (and children) would greatly increase the number of female converts.

As mentioned in the previous chapter, Western ideals of Christian womanhood placed a great importance on women as the centers of families and the primary purveyors of Christian faith (Wang, 2007). Women were believed by many late nineteenth-century Protestants to have a deeper and more mystical understanding of the divine. They were the cornerstones of Christian families, which in turn were the building blocks of Protestant communities. For this reason, many missionaries believed that the conversion of women was essential to the successful spread of Christianity, and most missionaries agreed that women could not be converted in China without the efforts of other women. Because of these "utilitarian" motives, some people have inferred that the Mackays' marriage was little more than a business partnership. Jane Lee, for example, emphasizes the fact that Tiu^n and her husband didn't celebrate their wedding with a party or pictures, or even a honeymoon. The first known picture of Tiu^n appears to have been taken four years after her marriage, and after she and her husband had already spent two years travelling around the world and preaching in Canada.

Figure 2 The earliest known photograph of Tiuⁿ Chhang-miâ. This image was first published in Mary Esther Millier MacGreggor's children's book, *The Blackbearded Barbarian*, 1912. The photo appears to have been taken in Embro, Ontario during George Leslie Mackay's first furlough sometime in 1881, probably before the birth of Bella Mackay.

In lieu of a wedding party and a romantic honeymoon, Tiuⁿ and Mackay immediately embarked on a tour of the Taiwanese mission stations so that everyone in northern Taiwan could see that Mackay had indeed lived up to his promise and married a native-born Taiwanese woman (Lee, 2014, 39). Mackay noted a significant increase in attendance at these services in his diary, and his letters home boasted that his new bride had substantially increased Taiwanese interest in the mission, *particularly* among women. It is likely that much of this initial spike in attendance was due to the novelty of their interracial marriage. While other Westerners enjoyed Taiwanese concubines or consorts, Mackay was the first to openly accept a Taiwanese woman as his legal spouse, and the interracial equality that this union symbolized resonated with the people of Taiwan, earning him the sobriquet "Taiwan's son-in-law".

Nevertheless, travelling with Mackay as an attraction was not always easy or safe. There were many people in Taiwan who saw the British and anyone who represented them as ruthless colonizers—enemies of Taiwan. Mackay was hit with animal feces on many occasions and at least once with a rock, and on one occasion, Tiu[n]'s sedan chair was attacked by a mob in Bang-kah, who threatened to burn it and its passenger alive. Only when the crowd heard Tiu[n]'s voice call out in Taiwanese cursing her assailants and begging for protection did they drop their torches and allow her and her husband and his students to pass (Mackay, diaries, November 17, 1889).

As mentioned above, Mackay continued to reiterate Tiu[n]'s importance to the women's mission throughout his career. When he wrote his memoir *From Far Formosa* in 1895 he placed special emphasis on his first meeting with Tiu[n]'s grandmother, Tan Thah-so, who became known as his first female convert. The importance of this first meeting later became the primary focus of a one-page biography of Tan Thah-so written by Tan Chhing-gi (Thah-so's grand-nephew and Mackay and Tiu[n]'s eldest son-in-law) as well as a page in Mackay's memoir despite not appearing in any of Mackay's early letters or even his diary. Mackay also devoted an entire chapter in *From Far Formosa* to defending the

Mission station	Pre-June 78 male	Pre-June 78 female	Pre-June 78 total	Pre-June 78 % male	Pre-June 78 % female	Post-June 78 male	Past-June 78 female	Post-June 78 total	Post-June 78 % male	Post-June 78 % female	All time male	All time female	All time total	All time % male	All time % female
五股坑	18	9	27	66.7%	33.3%	9	8	17	52.9%	47.1%	27	17	44	61.4%	38.6%
八里	15	6	21	71.4%	28.6%	14	7	21	66.7%	33.3%	29	13	42	69.0%	31.0%
和尚洲	15	5	20	75.0%	25.0%	11	3	14	78.5%	21.4%	26	8	34	76.5%	23.5%
錫口	14	2	16	87.5%	12.5%	51	19	70	72.9%	27.1%	65	21	86	75.6%	24.4%
大龍峒	24	15	36	61.5%	38.5%	33	7	40	82.5%	17.5%	57	22	79	72.2%	27.3%
艋舺	9	8	17	52.9%	47.1%	6	4	10	60.0%	40.0%	15	12	27	55.6%	44.4%
新庄	11	8	19	57.9%	42.1%	9	22	31	29.0%	71.0%	20	30	50	40.0%	60.0%
水返腳	15	2	17	88.2%	11.8%	21	7	28	75.0%	25.0%	36	9	45	80.0%	20.0%
紅毛港	1	1	2	50.0%	50.0%	18	4	22	81.8%	18.2%	19	5	24	79.2%	20.8%
Mission Totals	122	56	178	68.5%	31.5%	172	81	253	68.0%	32.0%	294	137	431	68.2%	31.8%

Source: Reprinted from Dodge, 2021, 90.

Table 1 Number of female converts in northern Taiwan

importance of the women's mission, in which he described the unparalleled success that native female preachers, like Tan and Tiu^n, were able to achieve (Mackay, 1895, 148, 297). While there were some skeptics, we shall see, who believed that Mackay's commitment to native "Bible women" was little more than a ruse designed to keep educated Canadian women out of Taiwan, by the end of the century it was widely accepted that the Canada Presbyterian Mission's success was due to its superior success at converting women, and most of this success was attributed primarily to Tiu^n.

A close examination of the mission's baptismal records, however, does not fully support the assertion that Tiu^n's marriage to Mackay instantly drew women to the mission. A tally of all baptisms performed at the nine mission stations that were open at the time of their wedding shows that the total increase in female membership after their marriage was only 0.3 per cent. While some communities experienced a large increase in female converts (the proportion of female baptism in Sintiam, for example, almost doubled) there were several others where the proportion of female converts decreased at the time (Dodge, 2021, 90).

All nine of the mission stations listed in Table 1 (from top to bottom: Go-Kho-khi^n, Bali, Hobe, Hsin-tian, Toa Liong-pong, Hsinkang, Hsinchuang, Ta^n Ma-ien, and Hongmao) were among the ethnic Fujian settlements around the Tamkang River in what is now Taipei and New Taipei City. This was the population that Mackay hoped would be most influenced by his decision to marry a Han/Fujian/Chinese woman which he later promulgated as the core factor in his success. However, this appears not to have been the case.

Most of the mission's three thousand converts, and nearly two-thirds of its female converts, came from indigenous Taiwanese communities in and around the Gilan plains, most of these evangelized in the late 1880s, long after Mackay's marriage to Tiuⁿ. The Fujian communities around Taipei followed similar demographic patterns to those seen in similar regions of mainland China. Women were sometimes baptized with their husbands (or their sons if they were widowed). The sons of converted men were frequently baptized with their fathers or at birth, but daughters were not usually baptized until their marriages had been secured. In many families (including Tiuⁿ's birth family) in which some members of the family became Christian and others did not, elder sons and their mothers who played important roles in filial rituals were often the last to convert (if at all). While the Canadian Mission was able to boast a greater proportion of female converts than any other Protestant mission in Qing China, most of these women came from the indigenous tribes that lived in Taiwan's central highlands and eastern plains—not from the Chinese communities of Taiwan's western coast.

The indigenous people of Taiwan were Austronesian peoples who had migrated to the island in successive waves over the previous fifteen thousand years. The earliest settlements were paleolithic hunter-gatherers who survived primarily on ocean foraging, but agriculture developed on the island by at least six thousand years ago. By the fifteenth century rice and sweet potatoes dominated much of the western lowlands of the island. The successive arrivals in the seventeenth century of Spanish, Dutch, and Ming Chinese settlers violently forced many of the indigenous people away from these prime agricultural and fishing territories into the central highlands and the eastern plains. In the 1870s, indigenous tribes still controlled more than half of Taiwan's land, and their relationships with the Chinese settlers and the Qing Empire were openly hostile (Stainton, 1999).

Taiwan's mountainous center and its windswept east coast were of little value in the seventeenth and eighteenth centuries. The central highlands had an abundance of lumber and game, but were difficult to farm and easy for indigenous peoples to defend. Along the east coast, the deep waters of Ryukyu Trench separated Taiwan from the rich fishing grounds of the Ryukyu forearc by hundreds of miles, greatly limiting indigenous people's access to them. At the same time, frequent tropical storms menaced Taiwan's eastern coast, making both fishing and rice farming much riskier there than at the northern and southern tips of the island or along its western coast.

The Qing divided indigenous tribes into two categories: the Pepohoan (熟番) and the Chhihoan (生番). The Pepohoans were "cooked" or "ripe" peoples who had settled villages that practiced agriculture and trade and were believed to be easier to be assimilated into Chinese civilization than Chhihoan people. The Chhihoans or "raw" people, on the other hand, were seminomadic hunter-gatherer groups less accustomed to agriculture and trade. They were regarded by the Qing Empire and various other colonial powers as unassimilable and a substantial impediment to Taiwan's development (Mackay, 1900, 92–96).

In the nineteenth century, demand for camphor and tea greatly exacerbated the relations between already marginalized indigenous peoples and the various groups of colonizers. Camphor, the

pungent pulp of a tree used both as a medicine and a key ingredi-
ent in smokeless gunpowder, was common throughout Taiwan's
central forests, while the best grades of tea could only be grown
at higher elevations in the mountains, where cool nights created
optimal conditions for better tasting tea leaves. The expansion of
these two markets in the second half of the nineteenth century
drew increasing numbers of Qing settlers into Taiwan's interior
to harvest camphor and build tea plantations. As Qing settlers
pushed further into the marginal areas of Taiwan, they waged
numerous campaigns to extirpate or eradicate the indigenous
peoples they encountered.

Periodic campaigns against indigenous peoples were nothing
new in Taiwan. During the first century of their rule, the Qing
suppressed more than forty revolts and waged twelve separate
wars aimed at eradicating Taiwan's indigenous peoples (Hung,
2000, 132–137). Many indigenous groups responded by wag-
ing intermittent war against the settlers. Frontier violence was
common and included head-hunting and ritual cannibalism
on both sides (Munsterhjelm, 2013, 84). Piracy of shipwrecks by
indigenous tribes was also common and led to substantial international pressure on the Qing Empire to subjugate or eliminate
the offending tribes. On several occasions entire crews were executed by Taiwanese tribes who captured them on their shores.

One such incident happened in December of 1871, when a fishing vessel carrying sixty-six Loochooan sailors ran aground on the
southeast coast of Taiwan. Only twelve of the crew were rescued
by Qing officials. The rest were executed by the Botans, one of the
more powerful indigenous tribes of the region. In 1872 Loochoo
was incorporated into the Empire of Japan, and the Japanese

demanded that the Qing punish the Botans for the massacre. The Qing response was that they did not control the eastern half of the island and so the Botans did not fall under their jurisdiction. After a year of inconclusive negotiations, the Japanese organized a six-month expedition into southeast Taiwan to exterminate the Botans themselves (Wheeler, 1903, 126–130).

Although the Japanese had many well-trained troops, they did not have any with experience in Taiwan's inhospitable climate. General Le Gendre, a former American Consul at Amoy and military advisor to the Meiji Empire, agreed to command the expedition along with several other former American military officers, and British steamships agreed to transport the troops. The Qing sent two ships of their own to monitor the initial landing, but raised no objections to the campaign for several months (Wheeler, 1903, 132).

Japan spent most of the six-month campaign scouting the area searching for the specific groups responsible for the massacre and negotiating with others for assistance. The Japanese killed at least thirty indigenous people in a variety of incidents but lost more than five hundred of their own to disease. Eventually the Qing objected to Japan's continued presence on the island and paid an indemnity of 500,000 silver taels to placate the Japanese and get them to leave (Wheeler, 1903, 168–169).

The Qing inability to prevent Taiwan's indigenous people from interfering with colonial commerce was perceived by other imperial powers as a major weakness, and the fear of tempting another invasion by appearing weak may have motivated the Qing to undertake even more aggressive campaigns against

Taiwan's indigenous peoples. Most of the powers operating in Asia agreed that Taiwan's indigenous people had to be eliminated. As E. C. Taintor put it at the 1874 meeting of the British Royal Asiatic Society in Shanghai, the indigenous people of Taiwan were "doubtless destined to disappear before the slow but steady advance of their more enterprising neighbors". The only question was, who would ultimately eradicate them, and when? (Taintor, 1874). In 1875, the Qing sent their own force to the eastern coast to suppress the Botans but were routed worse than the Japanese before them. More than 80 per cent of the Chinese forces were killed. In 1884–1885, the French would make another attempt to subdue the eastern coast during the Sino-French War, and also withdrew after suffering heavy casualties from guerrilla warfare and endemic disease. When the Japanese took control of Taiwan after the end of the First Sino-Japanese war in 1895, they initiated another series of systematic campaigns against the indigenous people, which continued through the end of the Second World War. Only recently have the indigenous people of Taiwan enjoyed some respite from this long string of campaigns against them.

Among these indigenous communities of central and eastern Taiwan, conversion patterns were very different from those in the Fujian communities of the western coast. Frequently, whole villages were baptized together on the same day. In these cases, every woman and child in the community would be baptized alongside the men. Often, because of polygyny and war, the number of women in the community exceeded the number of men significantly, and greatly increased the proportion of female converts to the mission. According to Mackay's diaries, in March of

1886, he, Giam, and Tan Ho (another Taiwanese minister from the Tan clan who was ordained with Giam at the outset of the Sino-French War in 1884) baptized 1,123 people together in eighteen villages over the course of just over a week, of which 752 of these baptisms are accurately recorded in Mackay's baptismal records held at Aletheia University archives (Aletheia University Archives, 馬偕博士受洗名單).

Unfortunately, not all of the communities listed in Mackay's diaries have corresponding pages in his baptismal records. The records that do remain in the Aletheia archives appear to be missing many pages, and a great number of the pages have been separated from their original bindings and become misorganized, making it impossible to account for every person that was baptized that week in 1886.

Table 2 lists fourteen villages that were visited in March of 1886 and the numbers of men and women baptized at each, constructed from Mackay's baptismal records. At least four of the villages listed in his diaries are missing title pages, and another four villages show discrepancies in the number of baptisms reported. Chin Tsu-li-kan (奇立丹), for example, has 143 fewer entries in the baptismal records (23) than in Mackay's diaries (169). Some of these may have been registered in nearby Ta^n Na-bi (打挪美), where the baptismal records show thirty baptisms in excess of what he reported in his diaries (46 and 16 respectively), but clearly many pages of these records have been lost entirely.

The original records were kept in small paper-bound booklets whose bindings have long since broken. Either Mackay or the editor-cum-ghostwriter, J. A. Macdonald, who completed *From*

Mission Station	Year	Month	Day	Males Baptized	Percent Male	Females Baptized	Percent Female	Total Baptized
Ki Lap-pan (寄立板)	1886	3	18	34	37.36%	57	62.64%	91
Bu-loan-sia (武暖社)	1886	3	18	20	71.43%	8	28.57%	28
Ki-bu-lan (寄母蘭)	1886	3	18	14	50.00%	14	50.00%	28
Tang-mng-thau (汁門頭)	1886	3	18	27	64.29%	15	35.71%	42
Lam Hong-o (南方澳)	1886	3	16	36	40.00%	63	60.00%	99
Pi-Thau (埤頭)	1886	3	17	45	54.22%	38	45.78%	83
Toa Tek-hui (大竹圍)	1886	3	18	11	42.31%	15	57.69%	26
Ki Bu-lau (寄武荖)	1886	3	17	64	60.95%	41	39.05%	105
Chin tsu-li-kan (寄立丹)	1886	3	17	7	30.43%	16	69.57%	23
Taⁿ Na-bi (打那美)	1886	3	17	21	45.65%	25	54.35%	46
Ta Ma-ien (打馬煙)	1886	3	18	42	62.69%	25	37.31%	67

Sau Heut (搵勿社)	1886	3	17	12	36.36%	21	63.64%	33
Pho-lo-sin-a-oan (浸腰莘)	1886	3	16	20	45.45%	24	54.55%	44
Hoan Sia-thau (番社頭)	1886	3	15	10	27.03%	27	72.97%	37
Total				363	48.27%	389	51.73%	752

Source: Compiled by the author from Mackay's baptismal records 馬偕受洗名單, Aletheia University Archives (1873–1899).

Table 2 Indigenous baptisms, March 1886

Far Formosa for publication, numbered each of these baptisms in pencil when counting them for inclusion in Mackay's memoir. Those individual numbers have helped to relocate many of the displaced pages that were inadvertently mixed in with the records from other mission sites. But the pages of these records were never numbered, nor was each page individually labeled, so there are many pages which could correctly align with the records of more than one village. A full and accurate accounting of Mackay's converts, thus, may never be known. My best reconstruction of the extant records is summarized in Table 2.

According to the extant records 50.8 per cent of the baptisms in the indigenous communities of Gilan were female, and the majority were children. In some areas around Keelung (基隆), the proportion of female converts was substantially higher. In the seaside village of Nanfang-ao, for example, the percentage of female baptisms was 63 per cent (Aletheia University Archives, 馬偕博士受洗名單). This is nearly twice as high as the 32 per cent of Fujianese converts that were female. This would imply that if Tiuⁿ's marriage to Mackay were indeed responsible for drawing more female converts to the mission, she attracted far more indigenous women to the church than women of her own Fujian-Taiwanese origin. While many young women came from these villages to Tamsui to study at the girls' school over the years, and Tiuⁿ was often entrusted with their care, it does not appear from Mackay's diaries that she played an active role in proselytizing these communities directly.

I hold that the gender ratios reflected in Mackay's baptismal records are more representative of the demographics of those villages that chose to enter baptism communally than of the influence of the Canada Presbyterian Mission's Bible women. For reasons that I will further elaborate in Chapter 6, the Sino-French War, in particular, drove many indigenous peoples to embrace the Canadian Mission, so in some ways it can be argued that the mission's disproportionately large female population was more the result of the French invasion than Tiu^n's popularity.

But even though Tiu^n's marriage to Mackay may not have resulted in the increased participation of Chinese women in the Canada Presbyterian Mission that Mackay hoped for, both he and the Canadians that supported him *believed* that it did. Their belief, and the imaginary founded upon it, led the mission to focus much of its attention on the education and proselytization of women. After Tiu^n married Mackay, more than a quarter of Canadian donations for the mission were earmarked for women's education, and after Tiu^n visited Canada for a year with her husband, speaking at dozens of churches, the proportion of donations to the mission that were specifically pledged for support of the "women's mission" rose to more than 40 per cent of the total. For the remainder of Mackay's career, the Women's Foreign Mission Society (WFMS) was the single largest benefactor of the mission in Taiwan, and the education and elevation of women were the primary directives associated with these contributions. The level of commitment to the women's mission was so substantial that Mackay often had problems budgeting for expenses outside of this directive and was called upon more than once to account for moneys that the WFMS believed had been improperly appropriated.

Of course, just because the gender ratio of converts did not shift in the way that her husband claimed it had does not mean that

Tiuⁿ did not affect the rate of conversion in northern Taiwan. The belief that Tiuⁿ's ability to draw converts to the mission was limited solely to women was part of the same mistaken imaginary that credited her for all the women who did convert. As the legal partner of a high-status foreigner, Tiuⁿ symbolized the imaginary of a Sino-Taiwanese equality with the West that was inherently attractive to many Taiwanese facing the threat of European colonization. Crowds came from all around Taiwan to see whether Tiuⁿ was real and listen to her speak. In Canada too, her ability to draw record audiences was noteworthy. It is altogether likely that Tiuⁿ was responsible for drawing just as many men to the mission as women.

Furthermore, twenty-four of the seventy-two male native preachers trained by the Canadian Mission during Mackay's lifetime were directly related to Tiuⁿ, as were at least five of the first fifteen Bible women (Ke Wei-si, 1899). While it is unlikely that Tiuⁿ was solely responsible for the disproportionate role that her family took in the formation of the Canada Presbyterian Mission, her family played a substantial role in its foundation. Tiuⁿ's nephew credited her with the direct conversion of her younger brother Tiuⁿ Sim-tiam, one of the early church's prominent native preachers (Zhang, 1987, 3). Her family also played a significant role in determining the direction of the church's growth throughout her lifetime. At the height of the mission, when Mackay boasted over three thousand converts and sixty mission stations, 60 per cent of the native lay-preachers had been recruited and trained in Tiuⁿ's hometown of Go Kho-khiⁿ. This meant that more than half of the native preachers who were not directly related to Tiuⁿ came from her village (Gamble, 2019, III, i. 56). Since each of these native preachers eventually chose the location to build his own mission station after he graduated, Tiu^n's clansmen and their neighbors chose the locations of most of the Canada Presbyterian Mission's outposts. In this way, Tiu^n and her family had a huge impact on the spread of the mission among Taiwanese men as well.

Perhaps more important than the quantifiable impact of Tiu^n's women's mission was the fact that Mackay and the Canada Presbyterian community *believed* that her ethnic gendered background uniquely suited her for success in this role. That belief led to the adoption of a strategy toward women's education that differed greatly from many other Christian missions in Asia. The mission relied almost exclusively on recruiting and training local Taiwanese women (mostly ethnic "Han", but also indigenous women) to work as Bible women, the female equivalent of the native preachers who were important auxiliaries in most East Asian missions. The decision to rely almost exclusively upon local women workers became very contentious in the Canada Presbyterian community. It also helped to tip the balance of power within the Taiwanese mission. Starting with the women's mission, the Taiwanese were able to exert their control of the mission to a degree that was unparalleled in any other nineteenth-century Protestant mission in the Qing Empire. By the time Tiu^n Chhang-miâ died in 1925, she and her children had more influence over the structure of the Presbyterian Church in Taiwan than the FMC, the WFMS, and all of the foreign missionaries these organizations had sent to "teach" them. In this sense, Tiu^n was a pioneering, contributing factor to the expansion of the Taiwanese Presbyterian Church and education for women on the island.

5
Tiu^n's first world-tour

To Canadians, Tiu^n Chhang-miâ was known as Minnie Mackay. Her husband told people that "Minnie" was short for Minerva, the Roman goddess of wisdom, a nickname reflective of Tiu^n's new Chinese name (which Mackay also gave her). Both the nickname and the story behind it were more memorable than her Taiwanese name to the Canadian readers of Mackay's monthly letters to *The Presbyterian Record*, a magazine devoted to tracking and promoting the global expansion of Christianity. Her new name and her almost miraculous ability to attract women to the Canada Presbyterian Mission were the first facets of a new public identity that Mackay would construct for his young bride.

Mackay's marriage to Tiu^n was publicly announced in a June 1878 letter to *The Presbyterian Record*.

> In May I was married to a Chinese Lady by the British Consul at Tamsui, and at once returned to the country to visit the stations with her. At every chapel, women who never entered the chapel door attended and listened to her sitting among them, telling the story of redeeming love.

> (*Record*, Sept. 1878, 241)

Mackay would repeat the narrative of Tiuⁿ's uncanny ability to draw and captivate female audiences wherever they travelled throughout his career. The same issue of *The Presbyterian Record* also carried another announcement—the arrival of two new missionaries in Taiwan: Kenneth and Mary Junor, doubling the mission staff.

In addition to supplying some relief to the tremendous workload of administering a church that now included ten mission stations, the arrival of new missionaries opened the possibility for Mackay to return home on furlough for the first time since his arrival in 1872. It was also a chance to take that honeymoon that both he and Tiuⁿ had been unable to. The Mackays delayed their trip around the world until their first daughter, Mary Ellen, who was born on May 24, 1879 was old enough to leave with a

MRS. G. L. MACKAY. FORMOSA.

Figure 3 Portrait of Mrs Mackay from *The Presbyterian Record*, September 1890, p. 245.

wetnurse. When they did leave in December of 1879, their journey took six months and included stops in China, India, Egypt, Palestine, Italy, France, and Scotland before arriving in Canada on June 24, 1880. By the time the Mackays landed in Canada, Tiuⁿ was already pregnant with their second child, Bella.

The decision to leave Mary behind during their two-year voyage home was an uncommon one. At the end of the nineteenth century, one local custom was not to bring a child outside of the home for the first six months of its life to preserve its health (much longer than the forty days Presbyterians traditionally wait before bringing a child to be baptized), but Mary was born in May, and was old enough to travel by the time the Mackays left. The decision to leave Mary with a wetnurse may have been a conscious effort to have a second child sooner. The prevailing view among Western doctors in the latter half of the nineteenth century was that health was directly related to the environment, and that acclimation to a particular environment was critical to surviving it. Mackay had already seen one Canadian woman and another Canadian child die in Taiwan of endemic disease and had survived his own near-death experience just a year earlier. He likely believed that leaving his daughter in Taiwan would help her to grow up resistant to the diseases there that were so deadly to foreigners.

There is no record of who the Mackays left Mary with. Singmaster claimed that they had left her with the other missionaries (the Junors), but there is no evidence for this, and it seems unlikely. If the Mackays left Mary behind because they wanted her to acclimatize to Taiwan, employing a nurse who was not herself acclimatized would detract from that mission. Furthermore, a collection of letters that was preserved by Mackay's aunt in Canada and donated to the Presbyterian Church Archives in Toronto in the 1980s reveals that neither Mackay nor his Taiwanese students trusted the Junors very much. A letter written by Giam Chheng-hoa and mailed to Canada while the Mackays were on furlough (CPC Archives 2009-5004-1-5, 6, 7, translated by Michael Stainton) asks Mackay what information he should or should not share with the new missionary. The same letter also reported that Mary was "OK and very good"—something that none of the monthly letters written by the Junors during the Mackays' furlough mentioned. The letter, along with a rough draft of Mackay's response agreeing with the opinion that Kenneth Junor should be trusted with as little as possible, leads me to believe that these missionaries could not have been entrusted with Mary's care.

The most logical choice for a caretaker would have been Giam and his wife, who were recently married and living and teaching in Go Kho-khiⁿ surrounded by Tiuⁿ's kinsmen, but there was another possibility as well. In the same cache of letters is a third letter, written by Tiuⁿ Chhang-miâ addressed to "Ma I-seng Niang" (the girl or wife of Dr Ma), the first English translation of which appears in the section Further reading 2. Previously, it has generally been held that Ma I-seng niang refers to the wife of Dr James Maxwell, one of the English Presbyterian missionaries who was stationed in southern Taiwan. The Mackays had visited the Maxwells in England on their trip home to Canada, and so Tiuⁿ had certainly met them, and may have indeed been "thinking about them ever since they left England". But the letter is written in POJ. Dr Maxwell certainly could have read it—he was one of the missionaries who taught POJ to Mackay—but it is unknown whether his wife, Mary Anne Goodall, who spent very little time in Taiwan, could have. Furthermore, a young woman from Handsworth, England would be unlikely to be impressed by Tiuⁿ's excitement at having ridden over snow in a horse-drawn sleigh.

An often-overlooked fact is that James Laidlaw Maxwell was not the only Dr Ma in Taiwan. There was also a Dr Mann living in northern Taiwan at the time. Hired by the British steamship company as part of the labor contract allowing them to mine coal in Keelung, Dr Mann of Nairn, Scotland supervised the conversion of the carriage-house where George Leslie Mackay lived before he married Tiuⁿ into the original Mackay hospital. For more than a year he volunteered a day each week to attend to sick people there. Dr Mann was one of the last people that the Mackays visited before they left on their furlough to Canada, and Keelung was one of their first stops after returning in January 13, 1882 (Mackay, diaries). If Dr Mann had married a Taiwanese Presbyterian, she might be the *Ma I-seng niang* addressed in Tiuⁿ's letter. But Dr Mann disappeared from the public record before the Mackays' return for reasons that may never be known. Even the Mackay Hospital Museum in Tamsui fails to acknowledge his contributions, despite the fact that they were widely publicized in the early 1880s.

The most likely possibility is that *Ma I-seng niang* was Tiuⁿ Chhang-miâ herself. After his acceptance of an honorary doctorate from King's College, Mackay (also known in Taiwan by the surname Ma) could also have been referred to as *Ma I-seng*, though he later came to be referred to, more appropriately, as *Kay Bok-su* (Dr Kay). Mackay, who spent a lot of his time distributing free medicine, administering first aid, and extracting rotten teeth, was often accused of using the title doctor to enhance his credibility in these amateur practices. The distinction between *I-seng* and *Bok-su* was made in part to clarify the fact that Dr Mackay was not one of many missionaries in Asia who had a medical degree.

If Mackay was the "Dr Ma" in Tiuⁿ's letter, then his "wife" (*niang*) would have been Tiuⁿ, and the sentence, "Goa' so Thia thang e Ma I-seng niu ai ho li tsai goa li" (translated into Mandarin by Robert Young as 我所親愛的，馬醫師娘要予你知，我離開倫敦至今有惦記你們不止) should not be read as "My beloved, Mrs Dr Maxwell, I would like you to know that I have never ceased missing you ever since I left London", as it has been in the past, but rather as "My beloved, Mrs Mackay would like you to know that I have never ceased missing you all ever since I left London". In this sentence, the "Ma I-seng niu" is Tiuⁿ herself, the subject of the sentence not the indirect object.

This interpretation of the letter leads me to believe that it was written in the hope that Giam would read it to Mary (the Mackays' first child), and perhaps others from her family, while Tiuⁿ was away. This might help explain Tiuⁿ's deeply emotional tone as well as her marvel at things like sleighs and snow that are magical to children and unheard of in Taiwan, but fairly commonplace among British subjects living in London, England, or Canada.

In this interpretation of her letter, the London referred to would have been London, Ontario, where Mackay had given the convocation speech at King's College less than a month before the letter was written (the same ceremony in which he was bestowed with the honorary title of Doctor of Theology). Furthermore, the fact that Tiu^n's letter was preserved in a collection of corre-spondence between Mackay and Giam Chheng-hoa leads me to believe that this letter was intended to go to northern Taiwan, and not sent with pictures of ice-covered lakes and snow to a woman Tiu^n had only met once in England, as has been previously suggested. Read as such, it is also easy to see the tremendous emotional cost that leaving her first child behind in Taiwan must have incurred.

The payoff for this difficult trip was the tremendous reception the Mackays encountered on their first furlough to Canada. Tiu^n and her husband were instant stars. Each week they visited three or more churches or home-based meetings to talk about their work in Taiwan. On Sundays, they often spoke to crowds that numbered in the thousands. Other nights they were guests of honor at smaller receptions of the Canadian elite. George Leslie Mackay was granted an honorary Doctor of Divinity for speaking at the 1881 convocation of Queen's University in London, Ontario and Tiu^n became a guest member of the WFMS and spoke with the ladies of the prestigious Toronto Literary Club, one of the first women's suffrage societies in Canada.

In my view, this is where Tiu^n made her greatest contribution to the mission. The latter half of the nineteenth century was a period of great religious optimism and philanthropic spirit. Amid the innumerable awakenings and revivals that spread across North America, there was a large market for sentimentalist literature, and inspirational speakers who could bear first-hand witness to the tragic conditions suffered by other peoples throughout the world. This narrativization of suffering began with the slave narratives that emerged at the beginning of the century. Powerful speakers like Frederick Douglass and Sojourner Truth travelled to Protestant church circuits in the northern US and Canada soliciting donations to help their cause. But enslaved persons were not the only oppressed people whose hardships garnered donations. Even while abolitionism was still gathering strength from the motivational power of real survivors, narratives of hardship from a multitude of diverse groups were regularly presented to Canadian congregations. To varying degrees, Ottomans, Indians, indigenous Americans, Greeks, Africans, and East Asians of all nationalities and ethnicities were presented to North American congregations as worthy of sympathy and salvation.

"Saving" these diverse sufferers was an integral element of the emerging narrative of Protestant triumphalism. Helping these wretched, who were seen as suffering from lack of *Christian* progress, was at least as important in the formation of North American Protestant imaginaries as it was to the health and welfare of the sufferers. The triumphalism of the "American Protestant Epic" (Sekora, 1987, 492) dictated that the subjects of sentimentalist narratives move through an arc from a pre-Christian (or uncommitted Christian) past filled with unimaginable pain and privation to a moment when help from a true Christian offers the opportunity of escape, the creation of a new life, and ultimately a life of pure Christian happiness.

According to Thomas Laqueur, this genre of sad sentimentalist tales had become stylistically fixed by the end of the eighteenth century, even as it grew more diverse and prolific over the course of the nineteenth (Laqueur, 2009, 34). The quantity and diversity of sentimentalist accounts grew, but the structure of the narratives changed little from the earliest abolitionist tracts. Laqueur suggests that this is because the subjects of these narratives are not really the sufferers depicted within them, but the readers who find their own salvation by vicariously experiencing the suffering of others, then giving their own labor and treasure to help ameliorate those others' suffering (Laqueur, 2009, 36).

Tiuⁿ's lived experiences included many events that could be fit into this sentimentalist mold perfectly. She had been "sold" by her family, then sold again. She had endured physical abuse and had tried to flee, only to be returned. Her mother-in-law had attempted to hobble her by binding her feet and had threatened and tried to kill her. Learning to read through the beneficence of the church and becoming a missionary's wife (one of the highest statuses achievable by North American Protestant women) clearly established the salvation arc in Tiuⁿ's narrative. Especially moving was the fact that most of Tiuⁿ's sufferings were inflicted upon her simply because she was a woman.

The Women's Foreign Mission Society of the Canada Presbyterian Church had just been founded in 1876 and had scarcely begun to meet before the Mackays' arrival in Canada in the spring of 1880 (CPC Archives FA-WFMS). The WFMS' stated goal was to "aid the Foreign Mission Committee by promoting its work among the women and children of heathen lands" (Presbyterian Church of Canada, 1876, 252). Most of the women on the committee hoped to achieve this goal by increasing the number and quality of the women who were working as missionaries abroad in conjunction with the FMC's work. Since the original charter only granted the WFMS the authority to raise money and allocate funds, it would be difficult for them to exert the kind of influence over church policy they hoped for. Still, the power to control funds was a significant step forward for these first-wave feminists. Their fundraising efforts began modestly with bake sales and quilting bees, but their accounts grew quickly. At the time the Mackays arrived in Canada, the WFMS had not yet decided how to use the money they had raised. The narrative of Tiuⁿ's lived experiences helped give them direction.

Many of the subjects/authors of early sentimentalist narratives were illiterate, and Sekora is just one of many scholars that have shown that these "autobiographies" designed to solicit spontaneous outpourings of emotional and financial support were often the product of significant ghost-writing by white Protestant editors. Because of this, both their historicity and perspective are subject to question. Even when professional writers exercise the strictest fidelity to the known facts, constructing a biographical narrative is not merely a process of transcribing a series of events from a person's life. Biographers invariably select facts, expound descriptions, and re-organize details according to dominant literary conventions in order to produce an alluring and understandable narrative. Authors choose when and how their narratives begin and when they end; they choose which experiences to include and which to leave out. They unavoidably emphasize those details that are important to their interpretation of their story and diminish others less in line with the narrative they are promoting. They impose upon their subjects' lives a dramatic arc that has a clear beginning, a rising conflict leading to a predictable climax, and a final resolution. Moreover, their narratives impose on events a thematic interpretation that explains *why* those events happened the way they are being described and *no other way.*

In the Protestant triumphalist narratives of the nineteenth century, heroes were expected to rise from a life of tortured despair through a long and dangerous journey in a perilous environment filled with dark and diabolical men who represented every form of sinfulness imaginable, until at last arriving at a moment of Christian awakening, where (usually) a single meek and selfless helper offers the hero a new education, a chance for rebirth, and finally a new "Christian" life that is simple, safe, prosperous, and happy. While the lived experiences of the heroes of early sentimentalist literature were undoubtedly fraught with environmental dangers, narrow escapes, sinful men, and even unexpected helpers, the narratives that were woven from these experiences often had less to do with the lived lives of the heroes within their pages than the underlying message that they were intended to support—that Christian faith and suffering with dignity were the only weapons men had to protect themselves from the evils of the world (Sekora, 1987, 488).

In the face of the demands of this sentimentalist narrative, even the most literate witnesses had trouble expressing their own experience in their own voice. Frederick Douglass, despite his erudition, was warned to supply "nothing but the facts". His editors would interject the philosophy (Sekora, 1987, 491). Tiuⁿ had won a prize for her writing by the time she was seventeen *sui* (the number of New Years she had lived in, the customary way of counting someone's age in premodern China), but never became the master of prose that Douglass was. She studied and taught POJ for fifty years, fluent enough in English to have published several letters to the WFMS in her lifetime, but never wrote a single account of her own life in her own hand. Nor did she ever give any public speeches that were recorded or reviewed except when her husband was there to interpret for her. During their first furlough, she was allowed to attend several meetings of the WFMS (to which her husband was not invited—she was reported as being able to manage "just fine" without his help), but the stories she told and the opinions she shared at these private encounters were not recorded.

On the rare occasions that Tiuⁿ was able to express her own ideas in her own words and be understood at the same time, those ideas were often dismissed as amusingly parochial, as when she asserted at their going-away reception that "she did not believe her countrymen were behind us [Canadians] mentally" (CPC Archives 2010-5006-1-2). As with Frederick Douglass' biography, Tiuⁿ's was always subject to outside editorial control. Her experiences may have been her own, and the alleged details might have transpired, but the broader narrative of modern womanhood and Protestant triumphalism that was crafted out of them came from the West, and was specifically constructed to justify the expansion of Anglo-American influence in China and Taiwan.

Throughout North America, a new imaginary of womanhood that is sometimes called the "Cult of True Womanhood" was arising out of the tension between first-wave feminists fighting for the most basic political and economic rights and the traditional Protestant patriarchies that had thitherto defined women's roles in Anglo-American societies. According to Barbara Welter, North American intellectuals and religious leaders began to promote a construction of femininity that held that "true women" were both the moral foundation of Western society and its most valuable treasure. According to this narrative, women's inherent virtues of "piety, purity, submissiveness, and domesticity" meant that women were the natural bastions of Western culture (Welter, 1966). Piety and faith were particularly seen as areas in which women were uncommonly gifted. While prejudices against women's intellectual abilities continued to justify barring them from ministry and other leadership roles within the church, the purity of their perfect (albeit simple) faith was seen as the most noble virtue for society to protect. This association of women with the divine, and with natural talents for nurturing the young and the sick, may have helped lead to increasing opportunities for women in religion, education, and health care. It certainly influenced the most important features to emphasize in narratives about the lives of women. In stories about Christian women, their successes as mothers, wives, and faithful followers were paramount above all other experiences.

The carefully constructed narrative of Tiuⁿ's early life fit the needs of these two narrative arcs well and proved to be a rousing source of sympathy in Canada's meetinghouses. Newly established organizations like The Toronto Literary Club and The Canadian Women's Suffrage Association drawn from a growing class of well-educated upper-middle-class women pressed for women's suffrage and expanded opportunities such as admission into Canadian universities. The founder of these two organizations, Dr E. H. Stowe, had been refused admission to the University of Toronto Medical School in 1865 because of her gender, and so had attended New York Medical College for women instead, and returned to become Canada's first female doctor, and its strongest voice for gender equity. Stowe was a Quaker (and therefore not a member of the Presbyterian WFMS) but spoke with the women of the WFMS on several occasions, and very likely met both Mackay and Tiuⁿ on their first furlough. For women like Stowe and her colleagues, the narrative of Chinese patriarchy served as a stark symbol for the inequities women faced everywhere, and Tiuⁿ's climb from child-bride and chattel slave to self-supporting young woman who had learned to translate Bible passages for a dollar a month and from there to the prized status of pastor's wife was an idyllic tale of the power of Christian womanhood.

During the Mackays' Canadian tour (and for many years before and after) *The Presbyterian Record* carefully tracked the donations received by the Canada Presbyterian Church as part of the evidence of the progress of Christianity around the world. Nearly every dollar that came through the church in the latter half of the nineteenth century can be found recorded among its pages. When Tiuⁿ and her husband arrived in Canada, *The Presbyterian Record* was read throughout 550 Canadian congregations hosting 174,134 members. In 1880 those members donated $585,844 to the church, of which $172,500 (or just under 30 per cent) was earmarked specifically for foreign missions (*The Record*, June 1880, 152). Mackay and Tiuⁿ's tour had a noticeable impact on these totals. In 1881, the Church balanced its budget for the first time in several years. "The marked increase in the funds for the year is doubtless largely due to…the powerful impression made by Rev. Dr McKay's addresses throughout the country" (*The Record*, July 1881, 187).

Some of these donations were supplied by wealthy benefactors, such as the widow of Captain Mackay of Winslow, Ontario, who pledged three thousand dollars to finance the building of a hospital in Taiwan to be named after her departed husband (*The*

Record, July 1881, 187). The bulk of the Church's support, however, came from the thousands of smaller donors immortalized in the magazine's acknowledgements. They included donors like the infants class at St Andrews who pledged one dollar and thirty cents to support mission work in Formosa, and dozens of local chapters of the WFMS who pledged three dollars each month to support the salary of a single Bible woman in her work in Taiwan (*The Record*, November 1881, 306). Together, the cumulative donations of 170,000 minor philanthropists amounted to what could be considered Canada's fifth most valuable corporate enterprise in 1881.

While Mackay did most of the travelling and speaking during this eighteen-month tour (Tiuⁿ, after all, was either pregnant or recovering from childbirth during most of the first year of their furlough), there is no doubt that Tiuⁿ's lived experience was responsible for inspiring a considerable portion of the funds raised. Of the $7,265 the Mackays brought back to Taiwan with them, $3,000 was the contribution of the widow Mackay from Windsor, and $1,800 was contributed by the WFMS (CPC Archives 2010-5006-1-2). By 1882, the WFMS would raise their pledge to over $4,000, and had insisted that this money be dedicated to the building of a school for girls in Taiwan. This girls' school became one of the most important goals of the mission and dominated the calls for donations that spread throughout Canada.

Mary Junor may have been the first to suggest the idea of a school for girls. While the Mackays were still in Canada, she wrote a letter to Mrs Harvey, the president of the WFMS, expressing her desire for a girls' school where she could teach (*The Record*, June 1881, 158). Restrictive gender norms made it difficult for Mary

Junor to join her husband in preaching to male-dominated congregations of northern Taiwan, and the reluctance of local families to invite a foreign woman (whose Chinese was not yet fluent)
into their home to proselytize women and children must have
made it difficult for Mary to feel like an active part of the mission.

Canadians, too, were still reluctant to invite women to participate in the governance and administration of churches and even
missions. In the WFMS charter, for example, women could raise
money and suggest how to spend it, but had no tangible authority unless supported by a directive from the all-male FMC. As
mentioned above, there was only one female doctor in Canada
in the 1880s and training programs in nursing had only been
available at select hospitals since the 1870s. Even opportunities
for women to participate in what men were insisting were their
"natural" roles as medical caregivers and teachers were extremely
limited. Mary Junor (and other members of the WFMS) undoubtedly saw the building of schools for girls not only as a benefac-
tion that would help save young Taiwanese women from the
abuses of traditional Chinese patriarchy, but also as an important
way of providing opportunities for educated Canadian women
to escape traditional Canadian patriarchy by embracing professional opportunities working in foreign missions.

The first donation to the girls' school was announced in the
September 1883 issue of *The Record*. Maggie Hall left a twenty-
five-dollar bequest "per her exrs [executors] for *girls' school at
Formosa*" (*The Record*, September 1883, 249). Margarette Hall, of
Dumfries, Ontario, died of cancer on November 9, 1882. She was
forty-one years old, unmarried and without children. She was the
owner of a small tract of land that had been part of her parents'

farm and lived there with her brother and his wife and family, who worked the land in conjunction with his own. She probably did not even know she was ill yet when she saw Tiuⁿ and Mackay speak during their furlough, but relatives said that she was greatly inspired by their story. Although Maggie Hall left ten dollars for "Dr Mackay in Formosa" (a donation which was acknowledged separately in the same issue of *The Record*), there is no mention of the girls' school in her will. The additional money for the girls' school was the idea of her sister and executor, Barbara Gowen, a board member of the WFMS.

The WFMS had just voted (quite controversially) to raise the money for a girls' school in Taiwan, ten days before Hall's will went to probate. When Gowen found that the sale of Hall's property left her with two hundred and fifty dollars more than expected, she quickly pledged twenty-five dollars of it to the girls' school on her sister's behalf, and had the pledge published in the *Record*, where, as the dying wish of a saintly woman, it could not be undone (Archives of Ontario, Reel 1, #389 file 1555 April 21, 1883). Before the Mackays had been back in Taiwan a year, the WFMS had added almost three thousand dollars to this total (Gamble and Chen, 2012, v2, 145).

Mackay and Tiuⁿ returned to Taiwan on December 19, 1881, and immediately began building. The hospital, Oxford College, and the girls' school were all finished within two years. Mary Junor, whose idea had led to the building of Taiwan's first school for girls, never got to teach there. Both she and her husband suffered from recurring bouts of malarial fever and left Taiwan for a restorative holiday shortly after the Mackays returned. Their four-year-old son, Frank, had died of malaria within months of their arrival, and they had never fully recovered from their loss. On top of sickness and depression they did not feel welcome in Taiwan the way Mackay had been. Neither of them appeared to have ever fully mastered Taiwanese and their letters to *The Presbyterian Record* intimated a condescending opinion of the Taiwanese that often bordered on antipathy. Within a month of returning from Japan, the Junors left Taiwan indefinitely. Several years later, a letter from the "North Formosa Church" listing seventeen (predominantly personal) complaints about the Junors' conduct was entered into the Mission record, and it was ultimately decided by the FMC that they not return (Gamble, 2015 s. I v. II, 119-21).

In August 1883, Mackay informed the FMC that the girls' school would be a boarding school, and he, Tiuⁿ, and the other native preachers would do the teaching there, and no Canadian women were needed to teach. It was a decision that would transform his and Tiuⁿ's image in the West forever. But first, there was another war.

6
The Sino-French War of 1884

"I never get tired of looking at the girls' school, it is so pretty," Tiuⁿ wrote to Mrs. Harvey on June 27, 1884. "In February last I went all over my native Formosa in the North and got girls to come to the school. Oh, what work to teach the poor girls from the East coast (not Chinese)…The thirty girls came dirty, wild, and could not read one letter; now they are clean, nice, and can read and write the Romanized colloquial".

(CPC Archives 1988-7002-2-3, 6)

The first batch of girls to come through the school were from mixed indigenous Peponoan communities from the mountains east and south of Tamsui. Their communities had traditionally subsisted on a mixture of hunting and farming in remote highland spaces that the Qing considered to have only marginal agricultural value. With the arrival of the tea industry in the 1860s and 1870s, arable land at higher elevations with southern exposures particularly well suited for cultivating tea became much more valuable. It became increasingly important for indigenous peoples in these highlands to learn to communicate and negotiate with the Fujian and British merchants who dominated the tea trade. At the same time, establishing cooperative relation-ships with these indigenous peoples became critically important to the peaceful expansion of that trade. It is unsurprising that the Canada Presbyterian Mission and its Tan allies sought students from these communities first. The first batches of students arrived with few possessions and little or no supplies with which to support themselves during their stay at the school, so Tiuⁿ had brought them to Toa Liong-pong by ferry to meet Li Chun-seng, the Fujian comprador who handled accounts for John Dodd and Tate and Co., two of the most influential British mercantile houses in Taiwan. In 1884, Li was still laying the foundation of his tea cartel, but by the time Taiwan was ceded to Japan he would be generally recognized as Taiwan's tea czar.

Li was from Amoy (Xiamen) originally where he had studied at an American Reformed Church school. There he had learned English so well that by the time he was eighteen years old he had become that city's most important comprador. He had also become a life-long devotee of Christianity. Li's personal, financial, and social support of Christianity may have been one of the most important factors contributing to Mackay's successes in Taiwan (Dodge, 2021, 46–58).

In 1884 Li donated uniforms and supplies for the girls' school's first class, who had arrived in Tamsui with little or nothing, and generously paid their tuition as well (Li, 1997, 4; Mackay, diaries, June 17, 1884). It was not his first donation to the mission, nor would it be his last. Over time it became a tradition that nearly every year either Tiuⁿ or Giam or both would present the school's students to Li, who in turn would encourage them with gifts and scholarships.

Although Tiuⁿ offered her thanks to the WFMS and shared the news of the girls' school's instant success as a celebration of the WFMS' hard work and charity, she unwittingly undermined one of the most important objectives of these women's work by assuming the lead position of head teacher in the new school. Mrs Harvie, the secretary of the WFMS, in particular had hoped that the girls' school would provide an opportunity for single women from Canada to teach in Taiwan. Tiuⁿ went on to suggest that her own job would become easier when Mr and Mrs Jamieson (two new missionaries who had recently arrived to replace the Junors) knew the language well enough to *assist her* (CPC Archives 1988-7002-2-3, 6). Although native teachers were common in missions throughout China and it seems that it was expected that Tiuⁿ would assist the women sent to teach at the girls' school, most missionaries considered these native teachers to be the assistants, subject to the direction of the foreigners they worked for. Tiuⁿ's assumption of superior status in her relationship with these new Canadian missionaries was a subtle reversal of the expectations that was reminiscent of her remarks questioning the superiority of the church homebase in Canada. Her letter would become the opening salvo in an eighteen-year battle with the WFMS over who controlled the mission in Taiwan. At the same moment another battle for control of Taiwan erupted—the Sino-French War of 1884.

Tiuⁿ's letter had not yet arrived in Canada when the French invasion of Taiwan began in August 1884. France had been attempting to build a sphere of influence in Vietnam despite local resistance for many years. France had de facto military control of several of Vietnam's southern provinces since the 1850s, but the northern portions of Vietnam continued to defy French colonization. In 1882, while the Mackays were building their new hospital and school, Henri Rivieri, a French commandant, attacked Vietnamese forces at Hanoi, prompting Prince Hoang Ke Viem to seek assistance from China. A prominent Fujian warlord, Liu Yongfu, entered Vietnam with his Black Flag army and waged an unconventional campaign that successfully halted French military progress in the region, and the French began seeking a diplomatic resolution to the Vietnam question. By June of 1884, the French had negotiated the Treaty of Huế with representatives of the Qing Dynasty, agreeing to divide Vietnam into spheres of influence between the French and the Qing. But the French did not have the military strength to enforce the terms of the treaty, and the Qing were either unwilling or unable to get Liu to withdraw his troops.

When Qing diplomats ended discussions with the French in Paris, Peking, and Huế, the French responded by attacking the Fujian navy and invading Taiwan in the hope of forcing a resolution. On August 5, the French navy bombarded Keelung and the next day marines landed. Their initial foray was quickly rebuffed, but on October 1 the French returned with 1,800 marines and captured the city. The Qing forces, led by Liu Yongfu's kinsman Liu Mingchuan, retreated strategically to the hills surrounding the port and besieged the French forces. Liu Mingchuan's unconventional campaign in northern Taiwan left the French forces surrounded in Keelung for six months, unable to make any progress into other parts of the island.

On October 2, the French began bombarding Tamsui in preparation for a second landing. Tiuⁿ and her three children (Mary Ellen,

Bella, and her son George William, born in 1882) hid under the floor of the manse during the shelling while her husband and her cousin walked the grounds nervously (CPC Archives 1988-7002-2-4, January 1889). The newly finished girls' school was struck by a French shell and badly damaged during the bombardment. The British remained neutral throughout the conflict but watched closely to study the tactics of both the Qing and the French. The British headquarters in Taiwan was at Hongmao Castle in Tamsui, on the same hill as the Canadian Mission, a fact which may have encouraged the French to be more reserved in their initial bombardment of the town. On October 8, the French landed six hundred marines in Tamsui, just a few hundred yards downhill of the mission, and tried for several hours to take the port, but were repulsed by Qing forces, who managed to capture a maxim gun in the exchange, which made it impossible for the French to advance against them.

Dr Johansen from the British Consulate joined Mackay at the mission hospital, where they tended to more than a hundred Qing green banner soldiers wounded in the battle (Mackay, diaries), an act of support that may have influenced Liu Mingchuan's decision to grant extended privileges and money to the Canadian Mission later on. After only six hours of fighting the British Consul, Alexander Frater, negotiated a temporary ceasefire and safe passage for any foreigners wishing to leave Tamsui before the fighting resumed. The French maintained the ceasefire at Tamsui for the remainder of the invasion, settling instead for a blockade of the harbor while they pressed their campaign from Keelung. The French never landed in Taiwan's third major port, Taiwanfu (Tainan today). Perhaps it was already clear from the events at

Tamsui that the French were doomed to be defeated both militarily and diplomatically in their attempts to assert control over Taiwan.

Tiuⁿ, the children, and the Jamiesons left Tamsui four days later for Hong Kong, where they joined English Presbyterian missionaries from southern Taiwan in safety. Tiuⁿ's husband remained in Taiwan incapacitated by fever. Mackay was allowed to leave the island and join them two weeks later, despite the French blockade. George Leslie Mackay and Giam Chheng-hoa appear to have been the only two people allowed to pass through the blockade once it was established, until it was lifted in April of the following year. Giam was allowed to pass through the blockade on October 15, 1884 by virtue of a handwritten letter from Mackay establishing that he was an ordained minister of the Canada Presbyterian Church, and its official representative in Taiwan. Giam went via launch from Tamsui past French warships to the steamship *Hailung* to retrieve ice to treat the fever that nearly killed Mackay (CPC Archives 2010-5006-1-1, 1888). Mackay was allowed to leave Tamsui on October 21 after he made a full recovery. He was the last foreigner to leave Taiwan after the French invasion, and on April 18, 1885 he was one of the first foreigners allowed to return.

On October 21, 1884, before Mackay was informed that he would be allowed to leave Taiwan, he wrote a letter to his wife to be sent out on the *Fukkien*. This letter, translated by Michael Stainton, served as a basis for his argument that Mackay's marriage to Tiuⁿ was not merely one of convenience, solely for the benefit of the church in Taiwan, but rather was based on true affection (Stainton, 2010). Mackay's salutation addressing Tiuⁿ as

"My beloved Chhang-mia" rather than the formal Mrs Mackay or Mrs M that appeared most often in his letters and diaries certainly was an uncommon show of affection on Mackay's part, and his detailed directions for the care of their children also indicate genuine concern. But the warning "no matter who wants to take the children swimming there, or somewhere else, you must be careful and not let them", reiterated later in the letter as "you must not scold the children there or let other people be in charge", highlights a paternalistic yet deeper unspoken fear, that Tiu^n's authority might be challenged or displaced by someone during Mackay's absence (CPC Archives 2009-5004-1-11).

Although Tiu^n was the undisputed matron of the mission in northern Taiwan, a fact which was well attested by Annie Jamieson's correspondence with the FMS, in Hong Kong Tiu^n would no longer hold the linguistic monopoly that ensured her importance. There were many foreigners in Hong Kong who read, wrote, and spoke Chinese quite well and a large number of Chinese Christians and businessmen who were just as adept at English as she. Moreover, most of the bilingual members of Hong Kong's civil society had the advantage of a much longer and more formal education than Tiu^n's four or five years studying under Giam in the old granary. The deficits in Tiu^n's background and education were sure to be much more noticeable in Hong Kong than they were in Taiwan or Canada.

Mackay urged Tiu^n to read Mathew 10:40–41 with the children:

> He that receives you receives me, and he that receives me receives him that sent me. He that receives a prophet in the name of a prophet shall receive a prophet's reward;

and he that receives a righteous man in the name of a righteous man shall receive a righteous man's reward.

Perhaps this was a scriptural reminder that Tiuⁿ was his representative in the exiled mission and spoke with his authority, as well as a cautionary warning not to let anyone else take charge of their children. Unlike many other exigent expenditures that were challenged by the FMC over the years and had to be justified with lengthy correspondence and detailed accounting, there is no record of the FMC questioning the cost associated with evacuating Tiuⁿ and her children from Taiwan to live in Hong Kong for six months. Still, the fact that they were the only native Taiwanese people allowed to leave the island during the invasion, coupled with the fact that she was not directly employed by the FMC, must have raised questions as to why she merited such a privilege. Ironically, despite her place in the elaborate Christian critique of East Asian gender roles that made Tiuⁿ such a celebrity in Canada, when separated from her husband abroad she too was subject to the bounds of traditional Eastern and Western patriarchies, in which her motherhood of the children of a man of importance was the critical guarantee of her status.

During those ten days when Tiuⁿ and the Jamiesons were settling into Hong Kong while Mackay was left behind in Taiwan, Mackay hastily oversaw the emergency ordination of Giam Chheng-hoa and Tan He, two of the mission's most respected native teachers. He claimed this was necessary in order to provide for representation and administration of the mission in his absence. These ordinations were ultimately confirmed by the Canada Presbyterian Church in 1887 despite the fact that ordination by a single minister without the support of a presbytery was quite unorthodox. Although Giam and Tan's status was in question for the first three years of their ministries, during the beginning six months of that time, they had sole and complete authority over the mission. After that, they were made voting members of the mission council, forever strengthening local Taiwanese input into the governance of the mission.

Their sojourn in Hong Kong did not help the Mackays' reputation. Unlike Canada, where local yeoman could scarcely imagine the exotic and orientified world of Taiwan, or in northern Taiwan where Dr Mackay was the best-educated Western man to be found, the British community in Hong Kong included many scholars who were both fluent in multiple dialects of Chinese and had earned doctorates in medicine as well as in divinity. Mackay found his methods challenged by more experienced theologians in many ways that left him humbler than he arrived, and the myth of Tiu^n's brilliance diminished slightly among missionaries better able to recognize her youth and lack of formal education. Mackay found that the opinions he had formed on evolutionary theory and providential design had gone out of favor in educated Protestant circles and he was introduced to the theological writings of Eduard von Hartmann as a corrective. *The Presbyterian Record* had noted that the "tide was turning" on theologies based on Darwin's new theory in August of 1884 (*Presbyterian Record*, August 1884, 212) and speculated that it would be difficult for learned men to continue to hold beliefs in both true religion and natural philosophy. Mackay, stubborn in his personal beliefs, continued to speak out against new interpretations of creation and divine design (Mackay, diaries, October 18, 1885).

Back in Canada a pseudonymous letter to the *Presbyterian Review* in the name of Philadolphus suggested that Kenneth Junor had been responsible for much of the work the Mackays had been credited with, and that having had his health restored and earned a degree in medicine, Junor might be sent back to Taiwan to help remedy problems in the Mission (*Presbyterian Review*, January 28, 1886, 2). Mrs Harvie, the secretary of WFMS, went so far as to publicly call Mackay's sanity into question, demanding to know what kind of a man keeps a count of the teeth that he has pulled? (Austin, 1994)

The French were not faring much better that spring. In six months, they had not been able to take any ground outside of Keelung. Although they only lost a few dozen men in the fighting, disease had killed almost half of their ground troops (Tsai, 2014, 102–103). In June of 1885 the French admitted defeat and began to withdraw. The Canadian Mission had been devastated. There was much unrest in the countryside during the war, and many Taiwanese did not differentiate between the French invaders and the other foreigners or their sympathizers who remained in Taiwan but had attacked foreign interests indiscriminately amid their resistance to the French. Many Taiwanese Presbyterians were attacked and robbed because of their relationship with foreign missionaries.

Governor Liu invited Mackay to present an account of the damages. Tiuⁿ's younger brother, Tiuⁿ Sim-tiam, wrote the complaint and presented it before Liu's court with Mackay. Liu ordered ten thousand dollars in silver paid to the mission. The complaint was handled as a missionary/church-related incident (*jiaoan*)—a complaint that Chinese Christians had been targeted with unlawful violence due to their Christian faith. The French did not ask for reparations or *jiaoan* payments after the war, probably because they had been embarrassingly defeated. Reparation payments, although common, would not have been appropriate since neither the British nor Canadians were directly involved in the hostilities. Nevertheless, Liu accepted Tiu^n's account that one Taiwanese Christian had been robbed of twenty thousand dollars by an anti-Christian mob as true and ordered ten thousand silver dollars restitution to be paid to the Canadian Mission. The payment would eventually be used to build four of the largest churches in Taiwan (CPC Archives 2009-5004-2-1 and Xie, 1997, 542).

Amid all the building and rebuilding going on in Taiwan, and disagreements with and even attacks on Tiu^n, Mackay and Tiu^n's ideology intensified. Their propagated desire to build a church that was governed by Taiwanese Christians rather than foreign missionaries was the focus of much criticism. Their assertion that all Christians were equal no matter their race or origin was particularly contentious back in Canada. "[T]he anti-Chinese cry which comes up from the whole western coast of America is gathering volume and awaking many echoes here in the East", commented the editors of *The Presbyterian Review*. "How shall we deal with the se [sic] heathen Chinese who are pouring in upon us is a pressing question which puzzles alike United States and Canadian philanthropists and politicians" (*The Presbyterian Review*, January 7, 1886, 4).

In response to a letter from Mrs Harvie of the WFMS questioning why Annie Jamieson did not assert more authority over the direction of the mission and insist that room be made for

Canadian women to teach there, Annie Jamieson admitted that she felt powerless to effect any change, although she appeared to contradict herself and support the Mackays in other letters.

> [I am] living here in my house with servants to wait on one. I do not come into contact with natives, but simply attend to my own sewing &c., which is little, read a little—English not Chinese—and occasionally write a letter to Canada. This is my daily life. I have never done more for the church.
>
> (Gamble, 2015, I iii 232)

Her letter understandably evoked a cry of outrage that manifested itself in a two-year campaign led by Mrs Harvie to have Mackay removed from the mission.

Mrs Harvie had been aware of Mackay's plan to operate the girls' school using native women teachers (he had repeated this sentiment in every letter he sent to the WFMS between 1882 and 1886) but she saw his decision not as an attempt to empower indigenous Christians but as a blatant attempt to prevent Canadian women from assuming their fair share of God's work. "We cannot…understand the special circumstances which make North Formosa the only field where the work of the foreign lady missionary cannot be employed", she wrote to Jamieson, adding later, "We also felt that if you were not so actively employed as perhaps you yourself had anticipated, it is only because the methods of Dr Mackay differ from those of ordinary missionaries" (Gamble, 2015, I iii 234–235). Annie and John Jamieson wrote many letters, perhaps voluntarily and perhaps involuntarily, defending Mackay's vision for a native church built by native workers, but these only seemed to have angered Mrs Harvie more. To Mrs Harvie's sensibility, Taiwanese girls were best taught by Canadian women, who were more naturally equipped to lead them away from the errors of their upbringing.

With Jamieson's help, Tiu[n] responded to Mrs Harvie in a carefully worded letter, half of which was published in the June 1887 WFMS leaflet.

> Our people are not like the Indians in the North-west and not like people in India, for I was there myself. Our people embroider beautifully themselves...the girls who attend receive Jesus just as girls in Sunday school at home do; there being very little difference. They are being taught what Dr. Mackay all along maintained they should be. Just what will make them better daughters, wives, and mothers. First, the Bible; Second, Reading and Writing in the Romanized Colloquial; Third making, repairing, and washing their own clothes, &c.; Fourth, preparing, weighing, and cooking food—kitchen work indeed!...Now do you think your Canadian ladies could do better teaching the above than our trained people here. I KNOW they could not.
>
> (Gamble, 2015, I ii 240)

Tiu[n] had previously suggested that if the women of the WFMS wanted to help teach Taiwanese girls to sew, they might do better by sending a shipment of sewing machines, which they had done in November of 1882. Now she reiterated her challenge to the WFMS' authority, saying that there was no need for Canadian ladies to teach how to knit stockings to "Chinese with bound feet [who] do not need". It has been suggested by some Taiwanese that Mrs Harvie was promoting the production of socks at the girls' school in the hopes of selling the merchandise for profit abroad, but it was more likely that the effort to promote Western-style socks was, as Tiuⁿ hinted in her response, directly linked to the campaign against foot-binding. Whether Mrs Harvie felt Tiuⁿ's opinion on the matter was irrelevant or offensive, her statements defending girls with bound feet were carefully excluded from publication.

Sensing that most of the Presbyterians in Canada did not fully appreciate the depth and ramifications of the debate, Annie Jamieson had her own pamphlet, *Some Facts about North Formosa Mission 1888*, printed in Hong Kong. In the pamphlet, Annie strongly supported Mackay's contention that foreign missionaries could not hope to be as effective (or inexpensive) at leading the mission in Taiwan as native workers could.

> I have gotten flattering letters from Canada referring to "glorious work" &c I am *supposed* to be doing while the truth is I am not doing what you call "mission work" at all; not even as much as I would do in Canada. And at the same time I see Mrs. Mackay from day to day, sometimes late at night, toiling away, while ladies in Canada know little, almost nothing of what she is accomplishing… Because she is a native and knows just how to deal with her own people, because she has mental gifts beyond those of ordinary women and because she has tact, common sense, good judgment, and warm sympathy, she exercises an amount of influence for good over all about her that cannot be understood by those who do not see her surrounded by Chinese.
>
> (Gamble , 2015, I, iii, 238)

Jamieson maintained that Tiu^n and other native teachers' fluency in the language, understanding of social conventions, and the respect and admiration they commanded from their fellow Taiwanese all made them far more capable of spreading the mission and expanding its influence than foreign missionaries could hope to accomplish. Ultimately, Mrs Harvie was unsuccessful in her attempts to have Mrs Jamieson replace Tiu^n as the head of the girls' school. Subsequently, she turned her efforts toward having the Jamiesons recalled instead.

Over the course of another year of heated correspondence, Mackay was able to convince the secretary of the FMC, Dr Wardrope, to overturn the Jamiesons' recall pending further review, and Mackay took care to make sure that his subsequent reports explicitly emphasized the work that they were doing. The movement to recall the Jamiesons was never revisited. John Jamieson died of tuberculosis on April 23, 1891 (Mackay, diaries). Annie was sent home to Canada a few weeks after her husband died. Now a single woman, whose POJ was not strong enough to teach at the girls' school, she was no longer considered an asset to the mission—a position that only reinforced Mrs Harvie's belief that Mackay's motives were overtly misogynistic. Jamieson returned to Canada widowed and having lost her only child during his infancy in Taiwan.

During the 1880s the peoples of Taiwan endured foreign influence and attempts at political dominance from multiple sources, be it Qing China, France, Japan, America, Great Britain, and other colonial powers in the Indo-Pacific region. At Tamsui and Keelung, local forces under the command of Liu Mingchuan thwarted France's attempts to seize the island by force. At the same time, the strengthening of Taiwan's tea industry's relations with Britain and America promoted an international climate that had limited sympathy for France's efforts. Liu's ability to repel the French while strengthening important economic ties with other foreign powers helped earn him a promotion to governor by Qing China, and the elevation of Taiwan from a sub-prefecture to a province separate from Fujian. While Taiwan was still subject to the Qing Empire, this was an important early step toward the establishment of a local government.

Within the Presbyterian mission, itself intimately intertwined with the international tea trade (Dodge, 2021, 193–195), the Taiwanese also scored significant gains toward self-governance. Despite the efforts made by some leaders of the FMC and the WFMS to promote a hierarchy within the mission that reserved primary authority to Canadian missionaries, by 1888, with the Canada Presbyterian Church's acceptance of the ordinations of Giam Chheng-hoa and Tan He and Tiuⁿ's elevation to matron of the girls' school, "native" Taiwanese Christians and their sup- porters had secured control of a majority of votes on the mis- sion council, and had established a controlling presence in the local governance of the Canada Presbyterian Mission to Taiwan, a reversed hierarchy to some extent.

7
A cooler homecoming

Tiu[n] and Mackay spent most of July of 1893 touring the fifty-six mission stations of northern Taiwan, saying goodbye. Mackay, who usually walked alongside his followers as a gesture of humility, joined Tiu[n] in matching palanquins. A great crowd of Christians and a band followed as they were carried from station to station where they were presented valuable gifts, culminating in a display of five hundred fireworks. A crowd of crying women met them on their return to Oxford College and begged them not to leave, but in August they auctioned off their personal belongings, donated one hundred dollars toward the building of four more mission stations (to round the total up to sixty), and set sail for Canada with their three children and a Taiwanese student intent on learning English (Mackay, diaries).

Officially, George Leslie Mackay was headed for his second furlough, and he and his family planned on returning to Taiwan in a few years, but the future was not certain. A few years earlier, Junor and his wife had left for Japan for a few months to recover their health, never to return. Mackay and Tiu[n] had been subject to much criticism since their stay in Hong Kong, and it was clear that the Reverend William Gauld, who had been sent to Taiwan to assist Mackay and relieve him for his furlough, should prepare himself to replace Mackay if need be. Mackay, for his part, had expressed a desire to educate his children in Canada in the hope that they might be immune to the criticisms that Tiuⁿ's lack of education had drawn, and he had been offered a lucrative contract to write his memoir. He also brought with him the collection of Taiwanese indigenous artifacts that made up his personal museum at Tamsui. If Mackay was not planning to retire in Canada, when he left today's Taipei with his family in August of 1893 he was certainly prepared for that possibility.

But the Mackays' second reception in Vancouver was not so welcoming as their send-off in Taiwan. Although British Columbia had welcomed thousands of Chinese laborers during the gold rush of the 1850s, and thousands more who helped build the Canadian Pacific Railroad, in 1875, a wave of anti-Chinese xenophobia known as the "yellow peril" led British Columbia to disenfranchise all Chinese Canadians and institute a forty-dollar poll tax for all Chinese persons trying to enter the province (Stainton, 2010, 3). The law was eventually stricken down by the courts, but the "yellow peril" only grew. Tiuⁿ had been admitted to Canada without question when she entered at Quebec in 1880. But just six months after her return home to Taiwan, America had already passed the Chinese Exclusion Act, barring unskilled Chinese immigration. Although Canadian courts eventually overruled the British Columbian poll tax and did not adopt a national ban on Chinese immigration until 1923, in 1891 most Canadians outside of the Canada Pacific Railway Corporation were in favor of excluding unskilled Chinese immigrants.

In 1885, Mackay published a scathing editorial in the *Toronto Star* in which he argued that Chinese workers had a right to live in America. In the article he argued that Chinese people's rights were protected by the fourteenth amendment of the United States Constitution, and that they were protected by America's 1858 most favored nation treaty with China. He also asserted that their rights were protected by God's law and the Bible. He further argued that the Chinese workers brought enormous benefits to America despite being disadvantaged with extra taxes and fees and other unequal treatments. The fact that Mackay's letter did not include any overtly anti-Catholic rhetoric, even though he had asserted such prejudices many times before, leads one to believe that he was unaware of the degree to which Irish immigrants competing with Chinese laborers for employment largely drove the anti-Chinese movement, but he did assert that Chinese immigrants were both more beneficial to the local economy and socially and morally restrained than other immigrant populations tended to be. In all Mackay's letter took up half a page of the six-page newspaper and was followed by a one-paragraph response reprinted from the *Stratford Beacon* that praised Mackay for being such a tremendous inspiration to Christians everywhere but noting that he had gone back to China and probably would never be back (UCC, 1885).

Over the next few years, while the Mackays were arguing for the recognition of the equality of Taiwanese teachers in Taiwan, the conservative party in Canada was fighting to pass a Canadian Chinese Exclusion act. Although Chinese immigrants were protected to some degree by the perception that their labor on the railroad was irreplaceable, in 1885 Canada passed its own brand of exclusion in the form of a fifty-dollar head tax assessed to any person of "Chinese extraction" attempting to enter Canada (Stainton, 2010, 14).

When the Mackays landed in Vancouver on September 26, 1893, custom officials there refused to allow Tiuⁿ and her children to enter Canada unless they first paid the fifty-dollar per person head tax. Mackay was infuriated and refused to pay the tax. Two local Presbyterians were able to convince the officials that Mackay's wife and children were British subjects, exempt from the head tax. These benefactors also paid the immigration fee for Mackay's student and future son-in-law, Koa Kau, on his behalf (Mackay, diaries, September 26, 1893). Once again, Tiuⁿ's lived experience radically altered the direction of her husband's ministry. Five days later, Mackay was on the pulpit at Mr Maxwell's Church in Vancouver, preaching against the unfairness of the head tax, and promoting the position that *Christians* everywhere were equal regardless of their race.

Although Mackay was just as prolific in his public speaking during his 1893 furlough as he had been in 1880, his reception in Canada seemed more reserved. His letters were still published and his speeches continued to draw large crowds, but correctives and explanations began to appear in *The Record* concerning some of his less orthodox opinions. In 1894, he was elected moderator for the 20th General Assembly of the Canada Presbyterian Church. It was the first time that a missionary on furlough had ever taken the presiding seat at a General Assembly in Canada, and it was rumored that he was awarded this prestigious position in part to limit his ability to comment on the floor during the convention. He had authored a proposal condemning the head tax and calling on the Presbyterian Church to advocate for its repeal. The strongly worded memorandum was not widely popular. Mackay broke with Presbyterian tradition and temporarily relinquished his seat as moderator to his predecessor, in order to give a fiery speech in defense of his proposal. No one spoke against him and no one else spoke on the motion's behalf either. The proposal was carried without a vote, but never acted upon. Mackay was permitted to proclaim his beliefs, then promptly ignored. *The Record* suggested that most Presbyterians believed it was not the church's place to get involved in government matters like immigration (Stainton, 2010).

Mackay returned to Zorra to settle down to write his book about Taiwan. While there was much enthusiasm for a book about his work, his publisher, W. S. MacTavish, B. D., did not appear to have much interest in the book that Mackay wanted to write. They disagreed about Mackay's focus on geography and his long defense of the "native church built by native workers", and ultimately, Mackay was forced to leave most of his notes with J. A. MacDonald, who became the book's editor and ghost-writer. Later, MacDonald claimed to be the actual author of *From Far Formosa* and even tried to exact a share of the royalties for this work from Mackay's estate, but failed (Rohrer, 2005, 11–12).

There are very few records concerning what Tiu[n] and the children were doing during this second furlough. Tiu[n] was granted permanent membership to the WFMS by virtue of a donation from St John's parish in New Brunswick. Anne Ross, Tiu[n]'s future daughter-in-law, remembered playing a game of crokinole with Tiu[n] and her children at a family party (CPC Archives 2009-5004-3-8). But Tiu[n] did not travel and speak with her husband as extensively during this second furlough as she had in the first. It is unclear whether this is because Tiuⁿ did not wish to speak to audiences or audiences were not as interested in listening to her. Either way, her opinions on these issues are unavailable in the record.

On April 17, 1895, Mackay was advised that his furlough would be cut short. Japan and Qing China had signed the Treaty of Shimonoseki, ending the First Sino-Japanese War. The First Sino-Japanese War was Japan's entrance into the league of imperial powers. Japan's primary response to the growing presence of Western colonial powers in East Asia had been the Meiji Restoration of the 1870s and 1880s, marked by the rapid industrialization and modernization of Japan's military, society, and government. During this period Japan also made repeated efforts to pressure Korea to open stronger trade relationships with Japan, including forcing an unequal trade treaty on Korea in 1877 modeled on the treaties that Western powers had forced upon the Qing after the Opium Wars. Japan sponsored a coup attempt in Korea in 1884 which ultimately failed.

The Qing Dynasty of China was also making efforts to modernize its army and reassert its long-held hegemony in the region. In 1894, when Korea erupted in the Donghak peasant revolution, both China and Japan sent troops to aid King Gojong of Korea. When those troops met, Japan and China ended up at war with each other and Japan quickly proved their military superiority both on land and at sea. Although Taiwan was far away from the fighting, Japan demanded that the Qing Dynasty cede Taiwan and its surrounding islands as well. The Qing initially refused and sent Liu Yongfu, the cousin of Liu Mingchuan and war-hero of the Sino-French War, to defend Taiwan. Japan landed an expeditionary force on Penghu Island in response and captured it in just eight days (Takekoshi, 1907, 81–82). The Qing officially ceded Taiwan to Japan.

The Presbyterian mission at Tamsui was thrown into instant turmoil. Margarette Gauld, the wife of the missionary sent to relieve George Leslie Mackay while he was on furlough, and all of the other foreign women in northern Taiwan were evacuated to Amoy, as they had been during the French invasion in 1884, but this time William Gauld did not go with the women like Jamieson and Mackay had eleven years before.

The memory of the looting that happened during the previous war created great anxiety in the mission, as did news of the massacre perpetrated by Japanese forces at Port Arthur (today's Dalian) in today's Liaoning Province of the People's Republic of China. While the British generally contended that the Japanese takeover would be a peaceful transfer, when the Chinese surrendered Lüshunkou just five months earlier, the Japanese forces under Yamaji Motoharu had slaughtered several thousand soldiers and civilians as punishment for the alleged ill-treatment of Japanese prisoners of war in Korea earlier on (Lone, 1994, 157). Many Han/migrant Chinese Taiwanese worried that similar reprisals might be carried out in Taiwan.

There also was a rumor circulating in Taiwan that the British were forming a syndicate with the intention of buying Taiwan from Japan (Hung, 2000, 164), but no such rescue materialized. Gauld reported on June 10, 1895 that "[i]t is also generally known that the natives of the Island invited Great Britain to take over the

Island and defend it against Japan. Britain refused to interfere. Then on the 25th day of May the Island declared itself an independent Republic, and the now ex-governor was chosen as the first President thereof" (Gamble, 2015 v5, 77). The British remained officially neutral just as they had in the Sino-French War a decade earlier, although they appeared to have leveraged their non-committal position to gain exceptional privileges, as they had in the previous invasion. The Japanese agreed not to interfere with the British consulate, its subjects, or any of their commercial or religious activities there, and so long as this remained the case, the official British policy was that the Japanese would administer and govern Taiwan much more efficiently than the Chinese had, so there was no need to intervene. William Gauld rented Giam Cheng-hoa's house in order to make it an official mission building and so Giam could obtain a British flag in the hopes that this would protect it from Japanese pillaging (Gamble, 2015, v5 78).

The consortium of Fujian-Taiwanese aristocrats resolved to form the Republic of Formosa included several veterans of the Sino-French War of 1884. Tang Jingsong (唐景崧), the third Qing governor of Taiwan, had led the Qing army in northern Vietnam and had been largely responsible for recruiting Liu Yongfu and his Black Flag army to support the Qing against the French. Liu had been very successful in his engagements against the French army in Vietnam, and there was reason to believe that he could defeat the Japanese army with the same tactics.

Liu and Tang hastily organized the Qing forces left in Taiwan and whatever native troops they could rally into a resistance army. Tang was proclaimed the president of the new Republic of Formosa and appointed Liu as Chief Commander.

Tang took charge of the forces in northern Taiwan, while Liu assumed control of the forces at Taiwanfu. The Republic of Formosa did not last long. The first twelve thousand Japanese soldiers landed on the northeast coast of Taiwan on May 29 and met the two thousand Republican skirmishers sent to defend Keelung on June 2. The Taiwanese commanding officer, General Chung, was shot in his sedan chair at the outset of the engagement, and the Taiwanese force quickly fell into retreat. Li Jingfang officially ceded Taiwan on behalf of the Qing Dynasty on a Japanese warship in Keelung Harbor the next day, and the Japanese occupied the port without further resistance. On June 4, Tang Jingsong and most of his provisional government officials fled Taiwan. Tang's army quickly turned to looting the government offices and the surrounding countryside (Davidson, 1903, 291–297).

A group of Taipei merchants sent a letter to Keelung, asking the Japanese to take control of the capital in order to suppress the looting. The Japanese took one outpost after another on their way from Keelung to Taipei. At Hobe Castle, famously built by Liu Mingchuan after the French invasion to be keystone in Taiwan's future defense, the Japanese were said to have entered unresisted, singing their national anthem. At Tamsui, home of the British consulate and the Canada Presbyterian Mission, a group of fifty-five armed foreigners, mostly Germans, assembled in the street and watched the Japanese army march through. By June 7, they had arrived at Taipei, where they found the gates to the city locked, but unguarded. One of the city residents passed a ladder through the gates which the Japanese used to climb the wall and secure the city (Davidson, 1903, 312).

Tiuⁿ and her children were far away in Zorra, Ontario when her home became Japanese, but her brothers and cousins were not.

Her younger brother, Tiuⁿ Tien-shi, was the teacher at the Bali Mission just across the Tamkang river from Tamsui during the invasion. He had just returned from a trip to Taiwanfu on church business when the Japanese came through. Unbeknownst to him, some of the church elders had taken advantage of the rapid retreat of the Republican army to liberate several boxes of rifles and ammunition from the Tamsui armory, which they stored at the Bali Mission station. A neighbor's child warned Tan just moments before the Japanese arrived to search the mission house, enabling him to lead Japanese soldiers away from the hidden weapons and thereby escape certain death. Later, he and his congregation buried the twelve boxes of munitions so they would never be found (Zhang, 1987, 3).

Liu Yongfu resolved to continue the resistance from the south, even after Tang's forces had lost the north. But by the end of July, he too had fled Taiwan, ferried to the mainland on the *Thales* disguised as a coolie (Takekoshi, 1907, 87–89). All that was left of the resistance were scattered holdouts and indigenous tribes who continued to fight a guerrilla war from the interior highlands. The initial invasion was swift and decisive. The Japanese lost only 164 soldiers on the battlefield. The subsequent occupation, however, proved much more costly for the Japanese. In the first six months 4,642 soldiers died from endemic diseases. Indigenous resistance to the Japanese occupation in the form of sporadic guerilla attacks continued right up through the Second World War.

The uncertainty of events called for the Mackays' immediate return to Taiwan, to help protect the interests of the Canada Presbyterian Mission there. The treaty of Shimonoseki provided Qing nationals in Taiwan a two-year window to sell their property and repatriate to the mainland if they did not wish to live under Japanese rule, but rather than leaving, the Mackays were returning. The fact that Tiu^n and her son, George William, both refused to enter in the Japanese household registry throughout their lifetimes seems to indicate that they never completely accepted Japanese rule. Both claimed Canadian status, and George William seems to have gone to considerable lengths to evade interviews with Japanese census takers later on. One oral tradition holds that years later, after George Leslie Mackay died, Tiu^n and her daughter Bella (who was born in Canada) tried to move to Canada with George William when he went to seminary but were not admitted. The only evidence of this is a letter from Bella's husband, Koa Kau, explaining that they had made the trip to Vancouver and safely returned, and a much later letter from the head of the FMC denying that it had ever happened.

Little else is known of Tiu^n's thoughts of the Japanese occupation. Although Tiu^n was now an honorary lifetime member of the WFMS, the conflict over the employment of Canadian women by the mission had ended their correspondence. Unlike the French invasion, of which Tiu^n's opinion had been published several times, Tiu^n remained silent through the Japanese annexation. Tiu^n's Canadian audience had found some humor in her comments about the French during the previous war but her thoughts about the British position (which was unofficially supported by the Canada Presbyterian Church) that Taiwan would be better off under Japanese rule were never made public. Tiuⁿ's younger brother and the Taiwanese Christians that he led submitted to the Canadian Church's policy of accommodation and discarded the weapons they had gathered to mount a resistance, but Tiuⁿ's life-long evasion of Japanese colonial authorities probably implies that she accepted this new status quo with her own consideration.

Only one letter written by Tiuⁿ during this time remains. In a note written in 1896 to her niece, Mary Ellen, Tiuⁿ briefly alluded to the increasing military presence of the Japanese, but spoke mainly about her garden, animals, and home (CPC Archives 2009-5004-1-16). Tiuⁿ also admitted that she had not yet returned to teaching at the girls' school . Tiuⁿ did not mention in her letter that Margarette Gauld had assumed control of the girls' school in her absence, and that the battle over whether the school was best run by foreign or native women was about to resume.

In the meantime, the Canadian Mission had become an important nexus for communication between the Japanese colonial government and the various people who inhabited their new colony of Taiwan. Mackay's diaries attest to the daily arrival of Japanese soldiers and officials at their Tamsui home. Mackay was able to meet with the new governor himself several times and negotiated special protections for Taiwanese Christians. At the same time the Japanese scoured Mackay's personal museum for intelligence about Taiwan's indigenous tribes and any other information that might help them secure their control of inland regions of the island.

Tiu^n graciously attended to her husband's frequent guests, but these new visitors were often less amicable than those that had come before them. Several Taiwanese preachers were arrested and beaten by Japanese soldiers during the first year of occupation, and one was shot and killed. The Japanese took control of several mission stations and used one meetinghouse as a stable for their horses. Soldiers began to attend services everywhere throughout the mission, bringing their own preachers and translators to lead discussions there.

The autonomy of the "native church" that Tiu^n and her husband had worked so hard to assert in the 1880s suffered a severe reversal in the 1890s. Mackay's assertion of the universal equality of Christians no matter their race, which had made him so popular in Taiwan, was not as well received in Canada. The FMC did not remove Tiu^n and Mackay from their positions, but sent new missionaries and began to implement policies it hoped might help restore Canadian control over the mission. At the same time, Japan assumed sovereignty over Taiwan, a development that met with support among a large part of the international community outside of Taiwan and Qing China. It seemed that much of the world agreed that the Taiwanese were better off ruled by Japan than by China, with no consideration at all for the possibility that the Taiwanese might be able to rule themselves.

8
You cannot live here anymore

In 1932, Tiu^n Chhang-miâ's daughter-in-law, Jean Ross Mackay, gave a Mother's Day radio address about Tiu^n. A typed copy of Jean's speech with hand-written annotations written by her husband, George William Mackay, is preserved in the Canada Presbyterian Archives (CPC Archives 2009-5004-3-10). The six-page address offered numerous examples of how Tiu^n's kindness, generosity, and faith made her a critical strand of the "three-fold human cord" that held the mission in Taiwan together. The address went on to especially praise Tiu^n for the humility she exhibited after George Leslie Mackay' death.

> Left a widow, while still a young woman, Mrs. Mackay wisely withdrew from all the activities which, up till then, had been her very life, and quietly took up her abode in a small house, a stone's throw or two from the white bungalow to which she had gone as a bride. The work of the Mission went on, under other hands, and she neither advised, nor criticized, but was ever an influence working towards harmony and peace. Not every successful worker has the grace to quietly withdraw, when circumstances alter, so as to make that the wisest course.
>
> (CPC Archives 2009-5004-3-10, second p. 4)

The May 8 radio address was delivered at a moment when the Second Sino-Japanese War, the conflict that would grow to become known as the Second World War , had already begun. Japan had occupied the homeland of the former Qing Dynasty (Manchuria, or Northeast China) in the fall of 1931 and declared the puppet-state of Manchukuo in response to an explosion along a little-used section of rail owned by Japan's South Manhuria Railway in the town of Mukden. Although it was later proved that Japanese soldiers detonated the September 18 explosion, Japan blamed the blast on anti-Japanese forces in Manchuria, and used it as a casus bello for their invasion. Japan went on to land troops in Shanghai in January of 1932 and killed more than eight thousand Republic of China (ROC) (1912–present in Taiwan, ROC) soldiers in the five-week battle that followed. Some scholars count the Mukden Incident and the subsequent invasions of Manchuria and Shanghai as the beginning of the Second Sino-Japanese War and the Second World War, but many Chinese scholars note that Japan's subsequent withdrawal from Shanghai and the ROC's decision not to defend Manchuria resulted in a five-year truce that lasted until the Marco Polo Bridge Incident in 1937.

International pressure from the League of Nations led to the signing of a ceasefire between Japan and the ROC on May 5, 1932, but Japan's troops had not yet been fully withdrawn from Shanghai when Mrs Jean Ross Mackay gave her speech. At this moment, when war in East Asia seemed ever more inevitable, Mrs Mackay mobilized the hallowed image of Tiuⁿ Chhang-miâ to reinforce Canadian leadership of the Taiwanese Presbyterian Church. The woman (Tiuⁿ) who had defied the WFMS probably consciously

and unconsciously in aid of (or used by) her Canadian missionary husband for whatever individual and collective purposes,
who asserted that Canadian women could not possibly teach
Taiwanese girls as well as native women, was now re-imagined
and promoted by a Canadian woman (her daughter-in-law) as
the paragon of humble obedience to her Canadian benefactors.
Tiu^n's abdication of the role of mother of the church and her
"non-critical" deference to its foreign leadership were offered as
models for all Taiwanese Christians to follow, at a moment when
the church's policy of support for the Japanese occupation of
Taiwan was growing more questionable.

It may be true that the Canada Presbyterian Church's support
of the Japanese colonization of Taiwan, just as they supported
the Qing Chinese/Manchu colonizers during and after the Sino-
French War of 1884, helped secure a much less violent tran-
sition of power. There was the modest resistance described in
the previous chapter, but the casualties in Taiwan were relatively
low (around 14,000) and the Japanese army never imposed
widespread martial law across Taiwan (Takekoshi, 1907, 88–89).
Although there were several incidents in which native pastors
of the Presbyterian mission had been arrested, and at least one
native preacher, Li Chioh-teng, was killed by Japanese soldiers
(Mackay, diaries, January 20, 1896), the church had remained
supportive of Japanese rule throughout the ordeal. In Bangkah,
an unnamed elder of the Presbyterian mission unilaterally organized a weekly collection among the tea merchants which was
used to purchase food, housing, and other supplies for the
Japanese soldiers, so they would not have to pillage as much to
support themselves.

Li Chun-seng, Taiwan's Oolong tea czar and wealthiest supporter of the Presbyterian Church, took a sixty-four-day tour of Japan with its first Taiwanese governor general, Kabayama Sukenori, in which they discussed their respective visions of Taiwanese modernity. These discussions resulted in the Taiwanese–British tea guild maintaining their monopoly on tea exportation, the capital of Taiwan being moved to Taihoku/Taipei and the centralization of internal transportation hubs there, and Li's appointment as counselor for Taipei.

In November 1896, Kabayama's replacement, Governor Nogi Maresuke (乃木希典), met Mackay and Rev. Duncan Ferguson of the English Presbyterian Church and promised that Taiwanese Christians, alongside foreigners in general, would be afforded official protection by the Japanese imperial administration. Orders were issued barring violence against Taiwanese Christians or commandeering their churches and mission stations, and providing for safe travel throughout Taiwan for the native ministers. Nogi was also deeply impressed by the fact that Mackay, a British subject, was married to a Taiwanese woman. Articles describing Tiuⁿ and her children appeared in the Japanese army news encouraging soldiers to go see her for themselves.

Japanese soldiers also began to patronize the church at Tamsui and other mission stations as well. At Tamsui, they often brought an interpreter with them to translate Mackay's sermons and add a homily and commentary in Japanese. The Japanese Presbyterian Church offered the mission three thousand dollars and the opportunity to join the Japanese presbytery and become an official part of the Japanese imperial religious organization, but the Canadians declined (Gamble,

2015, I, v, 84). Instead , William Gauld began making inquiries into the process for establishing a Taiwanese synod independent of the FMC. He and Mackay began meeting once a week with the mission's two ordained native pastors and Koa Kau, as an unofficial mission committee.

Mackay was in no rush to establish a more formal organization. Some speculate that his close personal relationship with the two native pastors and Koa Kau enabled Mackay to control the proceedings, and that he did not want to establish a real native presbytery if it would interfere with his control. Giam Chheng-hoa and Tan Ho, after all, were both from Tiuⁿ's adoptive clan at Go Kho-khiⁿ, as were Koa Kau and Tan Ho's son (Tan Chhing-gi, who would soon become Mackay's sons-in-law). Tiuⁿ was excluded from this new informal council, but so was William Gauld's wife Margarette—an arrangement which reduced the potential for conflict between foreign missionaries and the native faction and substantially limited Gauld and the Canada Presbyterian Church's influence over mission policy.

Furthermore, Giam, Tan, and Mackay together constituted the necessary quorum for ordaining future pastors, without seeking approval from the FMC as Mackay had had to for Giam and Tan a decade earlier. So long as there was no official presbytery in Taiwan, there was no venue for Gauld or anyone else to question their choices of appointments. But Mackay's precarious control over the mission and its future was quickly shattered. On August 8, 1898, Tan Ho unexpectedly died, and the native church lost its quorum of ordained ministers. Tan's son, Ching-gi, the top student at Oxford College, quickly stepped up to take over his father's work as the native preacher at Bang-kah, the largest congregation in Taihoku, but his ordination would not be approved until 1906.

The Mackays responded to this setback to the native church's autonomy by further consolidating the mission into their kinship networks. On March 9, 1899, Tiuⁿ's daughters were married in a gala double wedding on the twenty-seventh anniversary of her husband's arrival in Taiwan. Mary, the oldest, married Tan Ching-gi, and Bella married Koa Kau. With these unions, Mackay was now directly related to everyone on the mission committee except for William Gauld. He was quite literally the father of the church family, and Tiuⁿ was its mother.

Then, in 1900, Mackay was struck down with throat cancer. He died on June 2, 1901, leaving only one ordained native pastor (Giam) to represent the native voice in the Taiwanese mission. Tiuⁿ's children (and their spouses) would spend the next decade fighting to reclaim their lost control of the mission.

According to family tradition, it was just three days after Mackay's death—the day of his funeral—that William Gauld told Tiuⁿ she would no longer be able to live in her house. The manse, he explained, belonged to the mission, and since she was not a missionary and no longer a missionary's wife, she and her children would have to move (Margarette Mackay interview, 2014). To be fair, Tiuⁿ was not forced to vacate her home right away. Thurlow Fraser and his wife did not arrive to replace Mackay and Tiuⁿ until November 5, 1902, and did not move into the manse until Christmas Eve (Gamble, 2015, V, i. 67). The FMC suggested that Tiuⁿ, or even her son, George William, might be hired to teach at Oxford College or the girls' school so that they could continue to keep their life-long home, but although both options eventually came to pass, Gauld resisted both, and neither was expedient enough to keep Tiu^n and her family in their home.

Mackay was not buried in the foreigners' graveyard in Tamsui that had been built by his colleague Kenneth Junor for his son Frank so many years ago, but just outside of its wall on land the Mackays owned adjacent to the girls' school. Custom would not allow Tiu^n (and perhaps her children as well) to be buried in the foreigners' graveyard, so the Mackays started their own cemetery next to it, where they would all eventually be buried together. Many of Mackay's descendants have been buried there since, and even those descendants who have moved to Canada and America are memorialized there after they passed.

Figure 4 Photograph of George Leslie Mackay's funeral procession, June 5, 1901. According to Koa Kau, 451 people attended Mackay's funeral, 300 of whom were not even Christian.

In 1901, Tiuⁿ and her son George considered building their own house there, but a home like the one they had been accustomed to living in since 1879 would have cost most of their combined inheritance. Gauld, as executor of Mackay's will, refused to endorse the plan at the expense of George William's education. It was suggested that Tiuⁿ return to teaching at the girls' school, so that she could continue to live in the manse as a mission employee, but Tiuⁿ said that she did not feel ready, just two months after her husband's death, to resume that role again. Besides, Gauld argued that she did not really "know enough" to do the job effectively.

Contrary to the praise for Tiuⁿ's work that the Jamiesons had written a decade earlier, Gauld wrote, "she was never a Bible Woman; and so far as I am aware has not taught in the Girls' School. She was married to Dr. Mackay when she was a mere girl not yet out of her teens; and it would be very improper to employ such as Bible Women" (Gamble, 2015, v. 229–230). Gauld refused to turn over George William's inheritance to help build a house and instead arranged to have Tiuⁿ's son sent to Canada to further his education, so that he might become a properly qualified missionary before he took up employment in the mission. Gauld built a dormitory on the far side of the campus where Tiuⁿ could live with Bella and Koa Kau and their infant son. The building became known as Minnie's Tower (偕氏樓, Kaysilou). Koa Kau continued to work as the primary teacher at Oxford College, and Margarette Gauld became the first Canadian woman to take over teaching at the girls' school.

But Tiuⁿ's transfer to the reclusion of caring for her grandson in the college dormitories was not as humble nor as silent as her daughter-in-law later claimed. When Gauld would not hire George William to teach at Oxford College without further education, Tiu[n] and Bella and Koa Kau decided to move to Canada with him. Eleven years earlier Tiu[n] had been found to be a British subject by virtue of her marriage to Mackay, and Bella was Canadian, having been born in Ontario in 1881. Koa Kau did not have a claim to Canadian citizenship but had paid the fifty-dollar head tax in 1891 when he came with the Mackays on furlough to study English. The only documents that remain to attest to their trip is a letter from Koa Kau to the FMC describing their safe return from the voyage and an enigmatic note in Bella's obituary from 1970 that claimed she moved to Canada in 1902 never to return (Lai, 1972, 681). It is possible that Tiu[n], Bella, and Koa Kau were merely escorting George William to Canada, as he was still young at the time, but taking a two-week ocean voyage when the family's financial future was already in question in order to say goodbye in Vancouver rather than Tamsui seems extravagant for Tiu[n]'s tastes. There is no registry of immigrant arrivals in Vancouver prior to 1905, so it may never be known what happened at the border when she tried to repatriate to Canada.

We do know that by May 1903, Tiu[n] was once again working at the girls' school despite the fact that she "did not know enough", and that her reappointment was both the result and source of renewed conflict in the mission (Gamble, 2017, II, i, 38). Thurlow Fraser reported that the girls' school was the mission's worst failure.

> Our wealthy Christians send their daughters to schools on the mainland, and the poorer ones to Japanese public schools in preference to ours. As it now is except as

a boarding house for married students, in my opinion the school might nearly as well be closed. Mrs. Gauld deserves credit for her efforts to improve things, and has accomplished not a little improving the music in the mission. But in other branches her own education and her knowledge of the Chinese language are decidedly limited.

(Gamble, 2017, II, i, 61)

When Tiuⁿ was given a widow's pension of two hundred dollars a year plus a one-time gift of seven hundred dollars to cover the cost of the dormitory that William Gauld had built for her, Gauld suggested that she did not need to work in the school as a teacher anymore.

Attendance at the girls' school dropped to an all-time low, a fact that Thurlough Fraser attributed to the "disastrous consequences" of the Gaulds' rush to change the school's management. By the end of 1903 it had become apparent that the "Han"/"Chinese" Taiwanese were boycotting the school because of a widely held perception that Tiuⁿ had been forced out of her role as headmistress because of the Gaulds' prejudice against her. By 1904 the school was shut down (Gamble, 2017, II, i, 81–83). It remained closed until 1906, when Jane Kinney and Hannah Connell became the first two single Canadian women to work as teachers for the mission in Taiwan. Mrs Harvie's dream had finally come true (see Chapter 7).

Tiuⁿ and Mrs Gauld were hired back to co-administer the school and teach the new workers alongside a fresh batch of Taiwanese students. When the "Han"/"Chinese" community saw that Tiuⁿ was again in charge of the school the enrollment rose back to the levels it had enjoyed prior to her husband's death, and after she endorsed the two new teachers it did not drop again. By the end of 1907 the new teachers had passed their first language examinations and Tiu^n and Mrs Gauld retired together, neither to advise nor to criticize as others took over the work of educating young girls in northern Taiwan. Margarette Gauld left Taiwan shortly afterwards with her son, vowing never to return. In 1908, Tiu^n's daughter, Bella Ke, became the first woman in the mission to gain a Japanese teaching license, earning her the position of headmistress, and there was once again a Mackay at the helm of the girls' school.

It was not just Tiu^n's authority within the mission that the Gaulds seemed to try to limit. Rev. Giam was also pushed out of the mission's decision-making processes altogether soon after Mackay's death. Similarly, it took eight years of lobbying to convince Gauld to agree with the ordination of Tiu^n's son-in-law (and Tan Ho's son) Tan Ching-gi. Fraser often insinuated that Gauld's hunger for power was behind his alienation of native voices in the mission, but he might not have been intimately aware of the discussions of Mackay's sanity brought about by his unique commitment to a "native mission" that had led to Gauld's appointment twelve years earlier. Nor was he present in Taiwan during the first five years of Gauld's mission there, when William sat patiently as he was continuously overruled by a council of less educated men who felt that his voice held little weight precisely because he was a foreigner.

One of the objectives for Gauld had always been to reassert Canadian control over the Taiwan mission. He had advocated the establishment of a presbytery while Mackay was alive, in the hope that as more missionaries and teachers came to Taiwan, Canadian authority would eventually be reestablished. But when Mackay died, this step was no longer necessary. While Giam was still mourning, Gauld sent Giam home on sick leave and tried to close the mission station at Go Kho-khiⁿ. When other native teachers fell ill or retired Gauld hesitated to replace them, such that by the time the girls' school closed there were already nearly a dozen vacant mission posts. Fraser complained repeatedly to the FMC and fought to restore the native authority over the mission, but in the end, his wife caught malaria and they had to leave Taiwan. Fraser retired to write *Call of the East*, a fictional imaginary of how the mission *might have been* if Mackay had lived and he and Fraser had been able to work together. Still, the FMC either did not hear and agree with Fraser's complaints or simply tired of them. Gauld remained the head of the Presbyterian mission in Taiwan until his death in 1923.

The first Presbytery of Taiwan was finally convened in April of 1906, little more than a month before Tiuⁿ and Margarette Gauld retired. Not only did the elders ordain Tan as Taiwan's third native pastor but he was also elected its first convener (Jiaohui Daguan, 1972, 674). Tiuⁿ's son-in-law had become the new leader of the native church. In 1910, he and his wife Mary went to Japan for a year to study Japanese. When they returned in 1911, Rev. Tan applied to the Japanese colonial administration to incorporate the presbytery as the Northern Synod of the Presbyterian Church of Taiwan. The Northern Synod officially ceased to be a mission of the Canada Presbyterian Church and became an independent Taiwanese-controlled organization with a Japanese license. The original plan was for the Canada Presbyterian Mission to unite with the presbytery of southern Taiwan that had been established by the English Presbyterian mission to form the new Presbyterian Church of Taiwan (PCT). In 1912 the PCT was formed, and the English Presbyterian Church dissolved its southern presbytery, but the Northern Synod never dissolved its incorporation, for fear of losing their Japanese credentials. Today the Northern Synod continues to exist as a separate corporate entity from the broader PCT, even as it continues to participate and vote in that organization.

George William Mackay also returned to Taiwan from Canada in 1911, just in time to witness the building of the new Mackay Memorial Hospital in the colonial capital of Taihoku. G. W. Mackay returned as a fully ordained missionary of the Canada Presbyterian Church, complete with a Canadian missionary's wife. Jean Ross was a young woman from a prominent presbyterian family in Zorra who had known George since his father's second furlough in 1893–1895. A second-generation Christian feminist, Jean had the poise and authority to realize many of the dreams Mrs Harvie and the early women of the WFMS had fought for. G. W. Mackay was appointed to take over Oxford College, which was to be transformed into a college-preparatory school, while Gauld was to assume leadership of a new theological seminary being built in Shuang-lian in the capital, Taihoku. In 1912, G. W. Mackay resumed possession of the manse at Tamsui, eleven years after his father's death. Tiu^n was promptly moved out of Kaysilou, to take her "proper" place in her son's home at long last. Kaysilou was turned into a student dormitory.

Tiu^n did not stay in the manse long. In December 1912, she sat on stage with her children, Go Khuan-ju, the oldest living native

Figure 5 Opening ceremony for the Mackay Hospital in Taihoku, December 2012, Tiuⁿ Chhang-miâ's last public appearance. She stands just beneath the point of the flag, to the left of her son-in-law Tan Chheng-gi, convener of the Presbyterian Church of Taiwan.
Source: PCT archives, Tainan.

preacher in northern Taiwan, and all the missionaries, doctors, and teachers from the Canadian Mission in front of a crowd of over one thousand at the grand opening of the Mackay Memorial Hospital in Taihoku. Although there was a long program of Canadian speakers, Go Khuan-ju was the only native representative of the PCT invited to speak. G. W. Mackay, a Canada Presbyterian missionary now, gave the concluding benediction. This appears to be the last service that Tiuⁿ formally performed for the mission (Gamble, 2017, II, iii, 324). Her son-in-law, Koa Kau, was hired to become the head administrator of the hospital, and Bella became the principal teacher for a new girls' school of nursing and midwifery in Taihoku. G. W. Mackay, forced to conduct lessons at Oxford College in Japanese, went to Japan with his family to study language for a year. Rather than returning to the manse in Tamsui, Tiu^n took up a home with her daughter and son-in-law on the Jiancheng circle of Taihoku, a short walk from both Li Chun-seng's Oolong tea factory and the Tan family temple. They joined the church at Dadaocheng, where it is said that the congregation grew from fifty members to over four hundred within six months of their arrival (Li, 1997, 18–19).

9
Quiet resignation

In the last weeks of August 1925, George William Mackay visited Tiu[n] for the last time. He and his family, which by then included five children, were on their way to Japan for another year of studies. Tiu[n] still lived with her daughter Bella and her family in a small flat above a tailor's shop. Tiu[n]'s granddaughter Margarette remembered more than sixty years later that the stairs were so steep she had to climb them like a ladder, but then she was barely six at the time, and probably enjoyed climbing ladders more than stairs anyway (Mackay, 1989). Tiu[n] had suffered a stroke in the fall of 1924 that still wore on her face in their last family photo, though her doctors said she had fully recovered. A few weeks later, just days after her son and his family had arrived in Kyoto, she was stricken with a second, fatal, stroke on September 15, 1925.

Margarette Gauld had returned to Tamsui in 1923 for the mission's fiftieth anniversary jubilee, just in time to see Tiu[n] given a generous gift from the native pastors of the PCT, and to nurse her estranged husband, William Gauld, through the last months of his life. Canadians could "only imagine" how happy Tiu[n] must have been to see her old friend again after so long a separation (R. P. Mackay, Nov. 1924). Mrs Gauld stayed in Taiwan, and when Tiu[n] passed away in 1925, Margarette dressed her personally for the funeral so as to "spare her family the anguish of having

Figure 6 The Mackay family in the summer of 1925. Top row from right: Ke Weijie, Koa Kau, Tan Ching-gi, Tan Biyun, Tan Jinghui, Ke (Xiao) Meiyu (with child). Middle row: Bella Mackay, G. W. Mackay, Tiuⁿ Chhang-miâ, Renli, Mary Ellen Mackay, (unidentified). Bottom row: John Mackay, Xiao Kechang, Charles Mackay, Mingli Mackay, Xiao Meiwen, Margarette Mackay.

to do it themselves", while protecting them (and the church) from unfriendly gossip. One church member rushed to build a "Western-style" coffin for her with an open head so that only Tiuⁿ's face could be seen by all (Tan, 1925).

Her burial was delayed six days so that her son and grandchildren could attend. Hundreds of people came to say goodbye to her while she waited. On the day of her funeral, close to eight hundred people were in attendance (nearly twice as many as had come to her famous husband's funeral twenty-three years before). Tan Ching-gi gave the short eulogy, in which he described Tiuⁿ as a happy person, a peaceful person, and a kind person—the kind of person that everyone ought to aspire to be. Everyone concurred

Figure 7 Tiuⁿ Chhang-miâ's funeral procession, September 21, 1925. Aletheia Archives.

that she was indeed a great person. What manner of a great person, precisely, was (and is) still a matter for debate.

There can be no doubt that by the time of her death Tiuⁿ had become an important celebrity both in Taiwan and in Canada, but the nature of that fame is a little less clear. It seems that not everyone who recognized Tiuⁿ as a celebrity celebrated her for the same reasons.

For some, marriage to Tiuⁿ represented the dutiful sacrifice that George Leslie Mackay had been willing to make for the glory of the church. For others, she was a Cinderella princess, rescued from poverty by her marriage to the famous missionary. To those who sought to reimagine Christian womanhood she was portrayed as a quiet wife and loving mother, while Presbyterians in Taiwan saw her as the "spiritual mother" (靈性母) of their church (Lee, 2014, 39).

For Canadian first-wave feminists Tiuⁿ's lived experience was a glaring example of the helplessness of women under Chinese patriarchy that demanded feminine solidarity. She was the little girl who was brave enough to fight against foot-binding and a model of Protestant triumphalism—the heathen who after having been saved by the grace of God had gone on to save others.

For her daughter-in-law, Jean Ross Mackay, she represented humility and obedience in the face of adversity, but to her Taiwanese contemporaries, she represented a radical racial equality they believed most Canadians would never agree to, and to post-colonial scholars she has come to represent an even more radical indigenous challenge to colonial hierarchies of gender and race and the possibility of divergent indigenous modernities in Taiwan.

These narratives may not, of course, be the experiences that Tiuⁿ lived or even the events that happened to her, but stories—imaginaries—constructed by others in order to inscribe meaning onto the life that Tiuⁿ was said to have lived. Some of these imaginaries were conceived long before Tiuⁿ was even born. The "Spiritual Mother" motif, for example, is a construct that goes back not just to the beginnings of Christianity with its veneration of the Virgin Mary, but to time immemorial in the mother goddesses and harvest goddesses of ancient myth. Matsu, the young girl who gave her life to save her father and become a goddess of the sea, whose temple still stands on the bank of the Tamkang river less than fifty meters from the spot Mackay first landed in Taiwan, has long evoked the same "Spiritual Mother" imaginary.

Similarly, the "tortured life" of a Chinese girl was well laid out before Mackay met Tiu^n. He had read this story in Justus Doolittle's *Social Life of the Chinese* before he had ever arrived in Taiwan, and rewrote it in the narrative of Tin-a, described in *From Far Formosa*. Mackay's version of the narrative is vividly descriptive, but despite his personal acquaintance with many Taiwanese women, is based entirely on one who was admittedly fictitious. Although Mackay did not claim to be writing about Tiu^n's experiences, most of the narrative, with a few noteworthy omissions, was transferred directly to Singmaster's account of "Little Minnie".

One important difference between Tin-a and Tiu^n is that Tin-a, like most young women in Taiwan, was betrothed by the age of fourteen and married at fifteen. Mackay, however, insisted on waiting until Tiu^n was eighteen *sui* before marrying her. Singmaster extrapolated that since they were married in 1878, when Tiu^n was 18, she must have been born in 1860, and reported that "So greatly beloved was she in the city that the market dealers provided a large stock of food for New Year's Day, festival days, and Mrs Mackay's birthday" (Singmaster, 1930, 161). But Tiu^n's birthday was never officially recorded anywhere.

The first document that bears her age is Mackay's own Baptismal Record in which he listed her age as eighteen *sui* just a few weeks before he married her. Nor did he ever officially record her birthday. Mackay mentioned the celebration of Tiu^n's birthday twice in his diaries during their twenty-three years of marriage: once on December 4, 1887, and once on November 23, 1888. Jean Ross

Mackay noted on a prepublication transcript of the Singmaster biography sent for her review in 1928 that Tiuⁿ's birthday was November 21. Singmaster, perhaps realizing that this meant Tiuⁿ was not eighteen *years old* when she married Mackay as the biography claims, opted to leave the detail out.

Birthdays are a rather Mediterranean custom, celebrated in ancient Egypt and Greece and incorporated into Christian tradition with the adoption of the celebration of Christmas in the early fourth century. In most of East Asia, people's ages, until recently, were reckoned by the number of lunar years (虛歲 *xusui*) they had lived in. If Tiuⁿ was born in 1860, as Singmaster contended, then on January 30, 1861 she would have turned two *sui*, and on February 2, 1878 (the day before Mackay baptized her Chhang-miâ and recorded her age as eighteen *sui* in his baptismal records) she would have turned nineteen *sui* (years old). To be eighteen *sui* on February 3, 1878, Tiuⁿ would have to have been born in 1861, making her just sixteen years old when she married the thirty-four-year-old Mackay.

An anonymous biography of Tiuⁿ engraved at the Tamkang High School claims that Tiuⁿ was born on the twenty-second day of the tenth month of the lunar calendar in the first year of Qing Tongzhi. In 1887, the twenty-second day of the tenth month fell on December 4, the day Mackay first noted as "Mrs Mackay's birthday" in his diary. The following year, the twenty-second day of the tenth month fell on November 25, two days after Oxford College and the girls' school celebrated Mrs Mackay's birthday with a dinner party. Mackay left the following day on a long-planned three-week tour of the Gilan plain, so perhaps they had celebrated her birthday early because they knew he would be gone. If this was indeed Tiu^n's birthday according to the lunar calendar, then she would have been only sixteen *sui* (or fifteen years old) when she married Mackay. Qing Emperor Tongzhi's rule began on November 11, 1861, so the first year of his rule did not begin until January 30, 1862. If Tiu^n was born in the first year of Qing Tongzhi, then she would have been born on December 13, 1862. It would make her the same age as Mackay's fictitious Tin-a would marry according to Taiwanese custom.

If this timeline is correct, it would mean that the death of Tiu^n's intended and her adoptive mother's subsequent attempt to kill her that happened when she was ten *sui*, and the transfer of her care to her grandmother-in-law Thah-so, would have occurred during the spring of 1872, just as Mackay was beginning to preach in Tamsui. This was also the year that Thah-so invited Mackay to establish a mission in Go Kho-khi^n. Perhaps Tiu^n, like Tin-a in *From Far Formosa*, had hidden behind a curtain at the age of ten looking at her father's visitors through a crack in the wall while she remained unseen (Mackay, 1900, 298–299). It would also help to explain why so many people commented about how small and young she was during her 1880 tour of Canada, and perhaps why Mackay wanted to wait six months after their betrothal before marrying her. When Thah-so suggested she spend another half-year in the house to "pretty her up", it might not have been just Tiu^n's complexion that she was talking about.

While fifteen (or even eighteen) was significantly younger than the average age at which Canadian women entered into their first marriage (twenty-two) in Canada during the nineteenth century, teenage marriages were not unheard of. Tiu^n's unprecedented self-declaration of consent should have clearly established the legitimacy of their marriage. Moreover, the twenty-three years they remained together and the three children they raised clearly attested to the legitimacy of their union. So why did so many sources conspire to conceal her age while others carefully documented hints to reveal that deception? It was as if everybody agreed (albeit some begrudgingly so) to maintain the official narrative, but nobody really believed it was true.

Mackay's claim that he chose Tiuⁿ because she was the only suitable woman with unbound feet has led to similar ambiguities in the record. Most of the world was familiar with the practice of foot-binding, and the campaign to end it. The battle to end foot-binding was one of the most important objectives of Protestant missions throughout the Qing Empire. And Protestant missionaries, like Japanese census takers, were more likely to exaggerate the ubiquity of foot-binding than attempt to obscure it. Why would Mackay misrepresent the truth about Tiuⁿ's feet, and why would she spend fifty years maintaining that deception? Tiuⁿ had been willing to suggest that the sock-sewing skills of Canadian women were unnecessary for Chinese girls with bound feet, but even in her death, her family continued to conceal the truth about Tiuⁿ's feet. Her obituary reminded everyone that she had been an important leader in the movement to end foot-binding even before the Japanese outlawed the practice in 1895, almost as if to remind the public of the official narrative of Tiuⁿ's life. There are many touching stories in China and Taiwan about brave women who endured tremendous physical pain by unbinding their feet later in life to set an example for the younger generation of women they hoped to spare. Tiuⁿ could just as easily have been portrayed as one of these avant-garde first-wave feminists that suffered the pain of unbinding for the benefit of her children and her children's children. Instead, she and her husband (and their children) pretended throughout her lifetime that her feet had never been bound at all.

Perhaps they knew that the "unbound foot narrative" would unravel quickly. At the age of sixteen or fifteen, Tiu^n was not a wise old woman choosing to suffer stoically to save the feet of her grandchildren. She was a powerless adolescent being ordered to unbind her feet by a grandmother hoping to forge a new family alliance with her marriage—the same grandmother, perhaps, who bound her feet in the first place. She was compelled to unbind her feet for the same reason she had originally been compelled to bind them—to procure a more advantageous marriage. Tiu^n's family signed the pact of their shifting political and economic alliances on her body *twice*—the second time for the low price of thirty silver dollars (a bargain compared to the two hundred and fifty dollars Mackay later lent Tan He to procure his prized student's betrothal). This very likely was not the story that Mackay or his Canadian followers wanted to be remembered for, but it was a narrative that at least some of its Taiwanese witnesses did not want to be forgotten.

After she retired from the girls' school at the young age of forty-seven (or forty-five), Tiu^n only made a handful of public appearances outside of her own Taiwanese community. She spent most of her days sequestered in a small upstairs apartment in Taihoku. The Mackay Hospital has not kept any records of her treatment there, nor are there records left by the two Chinese doctors she was reported to have attended after her strokes. Japanese census takers never interrogated her personally and left the status of her feet undetermined, even while they investigated her children's claims to Canadian citizenship to some length. There is simply no way of knowing whether she chose to continue to suffer with the pain of unbound feet in her later life or not. Of course, others will point out that the narratives positively affirming her bound feet are equally suspect—an interview with Tiuⁿ's nephew sixty-four years after she died recounted stories his father had told him half a century before and a genealogy written *after* that. As Chen and Gamble pointed out in their respective papers fifteen years ago, there is no evidence that Tiuⁿ ever stopped binding her feet, but neither is there reliable proof that they were ever bound to begin with. All we really have are scattered anecdotes of Tiuⁿ's clumsiness, whispered gossip, and the fact that though her husband and his students routinely demonstrated their humility by walking barefoot around Taiwan, Tiuⁿ routinely travelled beside them in a palanquin.

Most people conceive of history as an attempt to prove what happened in the past. Students of history are trained to search out elusive points of evidence in diverse records, to interrogate each source for intentional or incidental biases, and present a clear argument proving what was the most likely succession of events. Laymen often imagine this process in the same terms that they imagine forensic scientists determine what happened from the scattered pieces of evidence left at a crime scene. But while scientists are adept at establishing certain facts that either did or did not happen, the story that is constructed out of those facts is usually not as definitive as the facts themselves. In the case of a crime, one lawyer may be able to construct a compelling narrative based on the undisputed facts that points to the guilt of a particular person, while another, equally skillful orator constructs a very different narrative from the *exact same facts*. Often, we can imagine hundreds of possible narratives that might adequately describe a given pattern of facts. If the facts themselves are in question, the number of potential narratives can compound exponentially.

In the distant past, much more than the courtroom, the provable points of evidence are few and the multiplicity of narratives adequate to explain their coexistence are many. Furthermore, unlike the courtroom, in which the intentions of the lawyers constructing opposing narratives out of the same facts are immediately apparent, the reasons why particular versions of past events emerge and are promulgated by others are often intentionally obscured. In the case of Tiu^n's age or her feet, I could speculate that the Canada Presbyterian Church sought to hide these details in order to protect the reputation of their most famous missionary (and their own) or that the Taiwanese, on the other hand, wanted to ensure that the world remember how powerless Tiu^n (and the Taiwanese themselves) were in this colonial moment, but these would only be speculations.

Even the undisputed facts of Tiu^n's life lead to the construction of a wide variety of conflicting narratives. This is partly because the details of her life are so scant. She wrote only a handful of letters, and is uncertain whether these were assisted or not. Her speeches were almost always interpreted and explained by others, and while she was often promoted as a spectacle to be looked upon and a model to be talked about, very few who talked with her reported back what she said or believed. The lack of details about Tiu^n's life and work have in fact made her life particularly malleable in its narrative potentialities. That her life can be simultaneously interpreted as proof both of the beneficent power of Protestant salvation and of the righteous resistance of the Taiwanese to Christian acculturation is strong evidence of the versatility of Tiuⁿ's imaginary.

But, although these narratives are very different, they are not necessarily mutually exclusive. People, after all, are inherently complex and multifaceted. There is no reason to doubt that Tiuⁿ was a devoted mother *and* a faithful Christian *and* a staunch feminist *and* a loyal Taiwanese all at that same time, *and* to differing degrees at different times throughout her life. One could even imagine that she was both a brilliant and studious young woman who was a naturally born leader *and* a scarcely educated colonial native whose ideas were largely ignored. She was probably both a staunch advocate for Taiwanese control of the Presbyterian Church and an obedient servant of the Canadian Mission who "wisely withdrew from public life" after her husband's death to support his successors.

To be effective as a missionary, Tiuⁿ had to be popular and respected among the Taiwanese. At the same time, to be acceptable to her Canadian benefactors, she had to represent both the moral decadence of Chinese customs *and* the superior Christian values that Canadians hoped to replace them with. In order to promote the outpouring of tens of thousands of Canadian dollars in donations each year, she had to be a victim that merited sympathy, but to be trusted with those donations she had to be a strong resilient leader. She had to prove that she could influence thousands of people for the Canadian Church to support her, but she had to prove that she was capable of resisting the foreign domination that the Church represented in order to convince people to follow her. Tiuⁿ's lived experiences were in many ways defined by the self-contradictory nature of the role that she was thrust into.

Like most teen icons, Tiuⁿ's public images were carefully crafted by her handlers. One of these, her own husband, had his own set of reputational demands to live up to. To justify his violation of one of the nineteenth century's strictest social taboos by marrying a woman outside of his race, that act had to be perceived as one of "self-sacrifice" for the greater good of God. In order for Mackay to be accepted by the Taiwanese he had to symbolically accept Taiwanese equality by legally marrying a Taiwanese woman and he had to marry a Taiwanese woman in order to acquire the local support his foreign prestige was based upon.

Luckily for Tiuⁿ and her husband, there were very few people in nineteenth-century Canada or Taiwan who understood both conflicting narratives well enough to compare the two. Tiuⁿ was young enough that her husband could attribute to her almost any qualities he wanted his Canadian fans to believe, and no one from the Canada Presbyterian Church other than Annie Jamieson mastered Taiwanese well enough to question his narrative until after he died. At the same time, Mackay's refusal to teach English at Oxford College and the disappearance of various letters and diaries kept most of his least favorable statements and opinions about out of the view of the Taiwanese public until long after he was gone.

There does not appear to have been any intentional destruction of historical records of the Mackay mission such as Alvin Austyn found in the archives of the China Inland Mission (Austyn, 2007), but there does appear to have been a concerted effort to manifest and maintain documents which would later support the narrative that Tiuⁿ and her husband (and the disparate communities that were their audiences) were endeavoring to construct.

Which leads me to my last, and perhaps most controversial, statement about historical narrative. Paul A. Cohen trifurcated history into the keys of event, experience, and myth, and held that it was the role of the professional historian to weed through subjective biases of people's experience and the intentional reimaging of mythologizers to reconstruct as close to a full and true understanding of the historical event as possible. People's lived experiences are limited by the finite nature of their knowledge and experience at the time of an event, and myths are limited by their intent to reorganize an event to support a preferred interpretation (Cohen, 1997). For Cohen, the processes by which events are experienced and mythologized occur at different times and are the result of the actions of different people. Those who were at an event experience it and transform it personally. Later, others who have collected the experiences of many mythologize those experiences by imbuing them with greater meaning. Only after that, with the benefits of hindsight and the broader perspective provided by amassing the experiences of numerous witnesses, can historians reconstruct and meaningfully interpret the past.

But Tiuⁿ Chhang-miâ's lived experience shows that history is not necessarily taking place in linear layers of increasing clarity. Tiuⁿ's life, we have seen, was mythologized long before she experienced it, and it seems likely that many of the events she experienced were intentionally constructed in order to reinforce the myths and imaginaries that she had been chosen to embody.

Her husband held a strong, if not clear, preconception of the meaning that he hoped his life (and that of his wife) would one day evoke, and chose his words and actions in accordance with the narrative he hoped his memory would evoke. Tiu^n's family, Tiu^n herself, and every other actor in this (and perhaps any) historical moment also had their own separate visions of the history they were hoping to create, and to some degree attempted to write the story they would live even before they lived it. Like many of us, they envisioned their future and actively attempted to influence it before it became their present, and long before it became our past. In many ways, the Mackays were prescribed before they even lived it.

In this way, I would argue that the imagination of history has as much of an impact on the unfolding of historical events as the events have on the eventual historical constructions that make sense of them. Experiences and imaginaries are not separate phenomena that happen sequentially in time-space, but rather concurrent processes that develop and evolve reflexively as people struggle to create meaning out of their lived experience.

Tiu^n's life and the diverse narratives based on it are perhaps particularly well-suited to demonstrate the double causality of experience and interpretation. She and her husband lived in a time and a place where political and social structures were constantly contested. The uncertainty of the future both empowered people like the Mackays to imagine bold new modernities and challenged them to prepare for unforeseen eventualities. Tiu^n and her husband's union in contested colonial space represented a unique syncretism of several of the nineteenth century's diverse cultures. Tiuⁿ and her husband lived a life that straddled these diverse societies and demonstrate that a more universal form of equality was in fact possible. To support and justify their position, they had to construct a variety of narratives to suit their diverse audiences. Together these narratives witnessed the emergence of distinctive Taiwanese Christianity, modernity, and the development of international relations between Taiwan and Canada. Whether event or myth, Tiuⁿ's narrative became part of these nation-building processes.

Glossary

A glossary of some of the terms that are used more than once in the book is provided here.

Hanyu pinyin Mandarin POJ	English
bainian guochi 百年國恥	"The Century of Humiliations"
daotai 道臺	toa-tai headman or magistrate
jiaoan 教案	a court case in Qing China involving Christian missionaries
jiejiao 解腳	unbind or "liberate" feet
nanwainünei 男外女內	Men manage the outer sphere, women the inner sphere
ninü 溺女	infanticide or "drown a daughter"
shengfan 生番	chih-hoan: "raw" or uncivilized indigenous people
shufan 熟番	peponoan: "cooked" or agriculturally capable indigenous people
simpua 童養媳	daughter-in-law
sui 歲	years of age
Wu Gukeng 五故/股坑	Go Kho-Khiⁿ N/A
yangmu 養母	adoptive mother
yangfu 養父	adoptive father
Zhang congming 張聰明	Tiuⁿ Chhang-miâ "Minnie" Mackay
zhennü 贞女	a virtuous widow
Zheng Chenggong 鄭成功	Koxinga N/A
Zheng Zhilong 鄭芝龍	Cheng Chih-lung N/A

Suggested Discussion Topics

Here are some questions to prompt discussion:

- Consider the degree to which people knowingly attempt to influence the stories that future historians will tell about their time? To what degree to people's perceptions of their historical legacy influence the real course of human events?

- How did the experience of colonialism differ in places like Taiwan and China where multiple foreign powers competed for influence as opposed to places Vietnam or the Raj in India where a single imperialist power claimed sovereignty over its colony?

- To what degree were the changes advocated by the Presbyterian Mission in Taiwan an extension of a foreign socio-political agenda and to what degree were they driven by the hopes and needs of the Taiwanese people themselves?

- Consider whether the Presbyterian Mission was more a tool used by foreigners to assert influence over the Taiwanese or one used by the Taiwanese to influence foreigners.

- Consider the degree to which Tiuⁿ Chhang-miâ, exerted agency in her own life, and the degree to which others controlled and constrained her agency.

- How should historians weigh the influence of "true events" in against the influence of widely believed "social imaginaries" when analyzing cause and effect in history?

- Compare the effects of Spanish, Dutch, Ming, Qing, British, Japanese, and French imperialism on the development of Taiwan.

- How has Tiuⁿ Chhang-miâ's life been variously mobilized as a symbol of modernity over time, and how has the narrative of her life story changed as to match the public's changing perception of modernity?

- In what ways does Taiwan's shared identity in the contemporary world shape divergent historical narratives of its colonial and pre-colonial past?

- Did George Leslie Mackay make Tiuⁿ Chhang-miâ famous or vice versa?

- How did Canadian women's efforts to educate and empower indigenous women in colonial space result in expanded rights and opportunities for women in Canada as well?

References

Archival sources: These have been cited with their author and date (where available), the name of the archive, and the archival accension number for the source. I have accessed the Canada Presbyterian Church Archives (CPC), The United Church of Canada Archives (UCC), the Aletheia University Archives (AUA), and the Mackay Memorial Hospital Archives (MMH) separately.

Andrade, Tonio. (2005) *How Taiwan Became Chinese: Dutch, Spanish and Han Colonization in the Seventeenth-Century*. www.gutenberg.org. Gutenberge: Columbia University Press.

Austin, Alvyn. (2007) *China's Millions: The China Inland Mission and Late Qing Society, 1832–1905*. Cambridge: William B. Ferdman's Publishing Co.

Austin, Alvyn. (1994) "George Leslie Mackay" in *Dictionary of Canadian Biography*. Vol XIII. Toronto: University of Toronto. http://www.biographi.ca/en/bio/mackay_george_leslie_13E.html (accessed April 16, 2024).

Bossen, Laurel and Hill Gates. (2017) *Bound Feet, Young Hands: Tracking the Demise of Footbinding in Village China*. Stanford: Stanford University Press.

Brown, Melissa. (2016) "Footbinding, Industrialization, and Evolutionary Explanation: An Empirical Illustration of Niche Construction and Social Inheritance". *Human Nature*, *27*, 502–532.

Chen, Meiliao. 陳梅聊. (April 2001) "*Maxie Jiaoshi Jiqi Jia Zai Tai De Shengya*". 馬偕教師及其家在台的生涯 [Teacher Mackay and His Family's Careers in Taiwan] in Taiwan shihua 台灣史話, 89–98.

Chiu, H. H. (2008) *The Colonial 'Civilizing Process' in Dutch Formosa 1624–1662*. Leiden: Brill.

Chuang, Ying-Chang and Arthur P. Wolf. (1995) "Marriage in Taiwan, 1881–1905: An Example of Regional Diversity". *Journal of Asian Studies*, *54*(3), 781–795.

Cohen, Paul. (1997) *History in Three Keys: The Boxers as Event, Experience, and Myth*. New York: Columbia University Press.

Convention of Beijing. (British Version) (October 24, 1860). https://worldjpn.net/documents/texts/pw/18601024.T1E.html (accessed December 24, 2023).

Copper, John F. (2014) *Taiwan: Nation State or Province*. Boulder: West View Press. [1975] 6th ed.

Declaration on Human Rights by the Presbyterian Church in Taiwan. (1977) https://china.usc.edu/declaration-human-rights-presbyterian-church-taiwan-1977.

Dodge, Mark. (2021) 臺勢教會: *The Taiwanese Making of the Canada Presbyterian Mission*. (*Tai Shi Jiaohui, The Taiwanese-powered mission*). Wilmington: Vernon Press.

Forsberg, Clyde R. (2009) "George Leslie Mackay, Miscegenation, and Mormonism: Having the Courage or Lack Thereof to Cross the Color Line for Christ?" A paper presented at The 2009 CESNUR Conference, Salt Lake City, Utah, June 11-13, 2009

Forsberg, Clyde R. (2012) The Life and Legacy of George Leslie Mackay: An Interdisciplinary Study of Canada's First Presbyterian Missionary to Northern Taiwan. Newcastle: Cambridge Scholars.

Hung, Chien-Chao. (2000) *A History of Taiwan*. Rimini: Il Cerchio Iniziative Editoriali.

Ion, Hamish. (2005) "A Case Study of Canadians in the Japanese Empire" in Canadian *Missionaries, Indigenous Peoples: Representing Religion at Home and Abroad*. Eds Alvyn Austin and Jamie S. Scott. Toronto: University of Toronto Press, 177–204.

Gamble, Louise. (2018) "Minnie Mackay: Taiwan's Hidden Treasure", unpublished essay.

Gamble, Louise and Chen Kuan-chou. (2012, 2015, 2018) *North Formosa Mission Reports Series I–III Vol 1–5*. Toronto: Presbyterian Church in Canada.

Ghosh, D. (2004) Gender and Colonialism: Expansion or Marginalization? *The Historical Journal*, *47*(3), 737–755.

Greenhalgh, Susan M. (1977) "Bound Feet, Hobbled Lives: Women in Old China". *Frontiers: A Journal of Women Studies*, *2*(1), 7–21.

Jordan, David K. (1997) "Chinese Matchmakers of Tianjin & Taoyuan", delivered at the Conference on Anthropological Studies in Taiwan Institute of Ethnology, Academia Sinica, March 21–23, 1997. Online at http://pages.ucsd.edu/~dkjordan/index.html.

Junor, Mary. (November 1879) "Formosa: Letter from Mary Junor". *The Presbyterian Record for the Dominion of Canada*, *IV*(11), 301.

Katz, Paul R. (1996) "Germs of Disaster: The Impact of Epidemics on Japanese Military Campaigns in Taiwan, 1874 and 1895" in *Annales de démographie historique*, Morbidité, mortalité, santé.

King, Michelle T. (2014) *Between Birth and Death: Female Infanticide in Nineteenth-Century China*. Stanford: Stanford University Press.

Ko, D. (1994). *Teachers of the Inner Chambers: Women and Culture in Seventeenth-Century China*. Stanford: Stanford University Press.

Ko, Dorothy. (2008) *Cinderella's Sisters: A Revisionist History of Foot-binding*. Berkeley: University of California Press.

Lai, John (1972) Elder John Lai's Archives. http://www.laijohn.com/index.htm has a strong collection of documents concerning the Presbyterian Church of Taiwan in Chinese, Japanese, and English. This precise article in Lai, "Church History Talks" (1972) No 681. Taipei: Presbyterian Church of Taiwan.

Lai Yong-xiang 賴永祥 (1990) *Lai Yong-xiang zhanglao shiliao ku*. 賴永祥長老史料庫. Elder Lai's historical materials. http://www.laijohn.com/Index.htm.

Laqueur, Thomas W. (2009) "Mourning, Pity, and the Work of Narrative in the Making of Humanity" in *Humanitarianism and Suffering: The Mobilization of Empathy*. Eds Wilson and Brown. Cambridge: Cambridge University Press.

Lee, James Z and Wang Feng. (1999) *One Quarter of Humanity: Malthusian Mythology and Chinese Realities*. Cambridge, MA: Harvard University Press.

Lee, Jane. (2014) *Maxie de "xuanjiao hunyin"—"Congzi" / "Congming"/ "Mine"xiaozhuan zhaiyao. Maxie chuanqi.* 李健美。馬偕的"宣教婚姻"—"蔥仔"/"聰明"/"蜜妮"小傳摘要.馬偕傳奇. ["Mackay's Mission-Marriage— "Little Onion"/ "Brilliant"/ "Minnie" a Summary of Sources" in *Tales of Mackay*.] Taiwan Tamsui: Zhenli Daxue, 30–61.

Li, Congxian 李聰顯, ed. (1997) *Da Dao Cheng Jiaohui 120 Zhounian Tecao 1875–1995*大稻埕教会120週年特艸 1875–1995. [The Dadaocheng Church, 20th Anniversary special report 1875–1995]. Taipei: Presbyterian Church of Taiwan.

Liu, Rebecca Karl, and Dorothy Ko (1972) Statement on Our National Fate by The Presbyterian Church in Taiwan – Motivation Based On Faith And Theology 1972. https://china.usc.edu/statement-our-national-fate-presbyterian-church-taiwan-motivation-based-faith-and-theology-1972.

Lydia Liu, Rebecca Karl and Dorothy Ko, eds. (2013). *The Birth of Chinese Feminism: Essential Texts in Transnational Theory*. New York: Columbia University Press.

Lone, Stewart. (1994) *Japan's First Modern War: Army and Society in the Conflict with China, 1894–95*. Palgrave Macmillan.

Lu, Weijing. (2009) *True to Their Word: Faithful Maidens in the Qing Period*. Stanford: Stanford University Press.

Mackay, George Leslie, D. D. (1900) *From Far Formosa: The Island, Its People and Missions*. Ed. Rev J. A. MacDonald. London: Oliphant, Anderson & Ferrier, 3rd ed.

Maeir, Charles S. (2000) Consigning the Twentieth Century to History: Alternative Narratives for the Modern Era. *American Historical Review, 105*(3), 807–831.

Mann, Susan. (2007). *The Talented Women of the Zhang Family.* Los Angeles: University of California Press.

Maragarette Mackay, unpublished letter, October 30, 1995 Tamkang High School Archives, Tamsui Taiwan.

Mitchell, James. (September 5, 2001) Memo to Epp Weldon. DFAIT doc. 665, 666, 667.

Munsterhjelm, Mark. (2013) "Mackay's Unburnt Legacy: Heroes-Rescue-Aborigines Organizing Narratives in the Exhibiting of Taiwan Aboriginal Artefacts". *Settler Colonial Studies, 4*(1), 82–99.

Olds, Kelly B. (2006) "Female Productivity and Mortality in Early-20th-Century Taiwan". *Economics and Human Biology, 4,* 206–221.

Pickering, William. (1898) *Pioneering in Formosa.* London: Hurst and Blackett Ltd.

The Presbyterian Record for the Dominion of Canada. Canada Presbyterian Church, Toronto (previously The Home and Foreign Record of the Presbyterian Church of the Lower Provinces of British North America) published monthly from 1861 [1876 name change] to December 2016.

Rejali, Saman. (2014) "From Tradition to Modernity: Footbinding and Its End (1839–1911): The History of the Anti-Footbinding Movement and the Histories of Bound-Feet Women in China". *Prandium: The Journal of Historical Studies, 3*(1), 1–10.

Rohrer, James R. (2005) "George Leslie Mackay in Formosa, 1871–1901: An Interpretation of His Career". *Journal of the Canadian Church Historical Society,* XLVII, 3–58.

Said, Edward W. (2014). *Orientalism.* Knopf Doubleday Publishing Group. Original publication date 1978.

Sekora, John. (1987) "Black Message/White Envelope: Genre, Authenticity, and Authority in the Antebellum Slave Narrative". *Callaloo, 32* (Summer): 482–515.

Shepherd, John R. (2011) "Trends in Mortality and Causes of Death in Japanese Colonial Period Taiwan" in *Death at the Opposite Ends of the Eurasian Continent: Mortality Trends in Taiwan and the Netherlands 1850–1945*. Eds John R. Shepherd, Theo Engelen, and Yang Wen-shan. Amsterdam University Press, 45–80.

Singmaster, Elsie. (1930) *A Cloud of Witnesses*. Cambridge: Central Committee on the United Study of Foreign Missions.

Stainton, Michael. (1999) "The Politics of Taiwan Aboriginal Origins" in *Taiwan: A New History*. Ed. Murray A. Rubenstein. New York: ME Sharpe Inc, 28–46.

Stainton, Rev Michael. (2010) "More Treasures Preserved Abroad: New Mackay letters in the Presbyterian Archives". York Centre for Asian Research and Canadian Mackay Committee. Paper presented Aletheia University, Tamsui. June 9–10.

Taintor, E. C. (1874) "The Aborigines of Northern Formosa". A Paper Read Before the North China Branch of the Royal Asiatic Society, Shanghai.

*Taiwan Jidu Zhanglao Jiaohui Beibu Jiaohui Daguan*台灣基督長老教會北部教會大觀 1872–1972. (1972) [Overview of the Northern Synod of the Taiwanese Presbyterian Church 1872–1972] Taipei: Presbyterian Church of Taiwan.

Takekoshi, Yosaburo. (1907) *Japanese Rule in Formosa*. trans. George Braithwaite. New York: Longmans, Green, and Co.

Tan Heng-Teng So, 陳雲騰嫂, "Tan Heng-Teng So Zhaogu A Chhang-A", Xu Qianxin gei Lai Yongxiang de han. 徐謙信牧師給賴永祥的函 [Tan Heng-Teng's widow's story about Chhang-A] in the original letter given to Lai Yongxiang by Xu Qianxin, jiaohui shihua, 194.

Tang Zhenan. (2001) 湯振安. *Taiwan Beibu Di Yi Jian Libaitang: Shejiao 128 Zhou Nianji Maxie Boshi Shishi Bai Zhounian Jinian Tekan.* 台灣北部第一間禮拜堂設教128 週年暨馬偕博士逝世百週年紀念特刊. [Northern Taiwan's First Church: 128th Anniversary, the hundredth anniversary of Doctor Mackay's Passing Memorial]. Taipei: Presbyterian Church of Taiwan.

T. C. G.（陳清義）寫 《台灣教會報》 488號 1925年 11月 p.5-6 [原文是白] Tan Ching-gi (1925) Taiwan Church paper number 488 november 1925, pp 5–6.

Tsai, Shih-shan Henry. (2014) *Maritime Taiwan: Historical Encounters with the East and the West.* New York: Routledge.

Wang, Dong. (2007) *Managing God's Higher Learning: U.S.-China Cultural Encounter and Canton Christian College (Lingnan University), 1888–1952.* Lanham, MD: Rowman & Littlefield.

Welter, Barbara. (1966). "The Cult of True Womanhood: 1820–1860". *American Quarterly*, *18*(2), 151–174.

Wheeler, James Davidson. (1903) *The Island of Formosa, Past and Present. History, people, resources, and commercial prospects. Tea, camphor, sugar, gold, coal, sulphur, economical plants, and other productions.* London: Macmillan and Co.

Xie Jialiang, 谢嘉梁 (1997) "Fa Jun Qin Tai Dang Xia" in *Taiwan Lishi Wen Xian Cong Kan.* 法軍侵臺檔下 臺灣歷史文獻灘刊 ["Files on the French Invasion of Taiwan" in *Taiwan History Collection*]. Taipei: Taiwan Shengwen Xianwei Yuanhu, 542.

Zhang, Tanhui, ed. 張炎輝敬編 (2006) *Zhang Huari Zupu di Wufang Ershishi Yisun*張華日族譜第五房二十世裔孫, [The Zhang Sunflower Genealogy, 5th generation including the 20th century], family-published.

Zhang, Yuehan. 張約翰. (1987) Shang Zhu Da Neng gujin Xian Xianzai Xin Zhu ZhiJia. 上主大能古今顯現在信主之家. [The story of our family's faith in God, from ancient times to today]. April 1987. Handwritten manuscript courtesy of Jaffa Chang, granddaughter of Zhang Yuehan.

Further reading 1a

Zhang (Tiuⁿ) Yuehan's account of the Early Church (1–3)

上主大能古今顯現在信主之家

張約翰紀錄
一九八七年民國七十六年四月

上主的救恩宰我卑徽家

P1

我的原籍在五股坑內. 阿公張忠生有三男一女家父. 新天
有一位哥哥也有一位弟弟.有一位妹妹名蔥仔. 在北部風
俗女兒自幼份給五股坑口. 一位只生孤子將來成人要匹
配作夫婦. 我的阿媽就托人份一位女兒. 要配給家父. 一
段時間阿姑12 [sic] 雖是她的對上生病來離開世間對那
時起養母開始非常逆待說妳是破格一位對上給妳破破
死.就用種種方法來逆待. 一天要擎二斗乾落花生(土豆)
擎到手非常疼痛過年29 晚只有食菜尾. 我的母親對我說
有一次下大雨給養母打去盡利害半夜逃走回來生母家
裏.叫門時我的阿媽叫大伯取一破椶簑給她再回去養母
家. 有大嬸建議說現在下大雨應該給她入內洗[澡]換衣
服待明天實情如何[與]大伯找回去養母家.阿無有主的道
理連親生女兒都無有愛心.後來回去養母家.每日口講不
出的[原]苦來過日亲得上帝保護身体有主的庇佑健康到
十五歲時.馬偕博士起初來[臺]創設牛律大學(現台灣神
學院)並創設醫[管](現馬偕紀念醫院)來栮清病痛內体上
痛苦以及牙科.也來招呼學生功讀牛律大學培養傳道人
材. 一方面募集[醫]療助手養成醫療人員. 又以方面傳耶

穌基督的福音在各地方.所以為着主的福音傳到五股坑
口來招呼不論男女孩子來讀羅馬字(白話字) 連連招一個
餘月無有一人來讀後來馬偕博士就出告示若有十二歲
以上男女小孩願意來讀著每個月要發一元白銀(當然清
時代一斗白米二角左右錢)告示出去了到禮拜天朝起時
全五股坑口所有十二歲以上阿姑也在

P2

內已有百餘人來報名讀白話字也教他們吟養心新詩(現聖
詩)也做禮拜敬畏上帝.一方面也從基督的福音傳給他們.
百餘名學生其中阿姑讀了成[績]最好.到一段時間大家努
力功讀也已[經]都會讀新舊約聖[經]了因為阿姑會賺錢養
母就無再逆待.[經]過一段時間馬偕博士要回去祖國加拿
大項母會種種報告來回當時交通不便需要半年久就吩咐
學生講他回來時要向你們測驗在新舊約聖經限開一人讀
一章讀了最好者為荣一名獎三元白銀二名獎二元三名壹
願百餘名學生其中阿姑讀了最好就獎三元白銀取回去給
養母時非常歡喜. 在此時阿姑已十七歲了. 牛律學生問馬
偕博士你有意要同化嗎, 說有意 學生再問是誰你定意.說
張蔥因為她真聰明. 牛律學生說去向養母作親事. 養母就
答應.　馬偕博士就送聘禮金三十元白銀又說者婚後每個
月扶養金三元白銀領到她百年歲後.馬偕博士用主的福
音種種好款待他養母的心受感動也來信主耶穌是五古
坑教會第一代女信走,　阿姑十八歲時與馬偕博士結婚馬
偕摯時就改阿姑的名張聰明(結婚禮服現保存在北部大
會)婚後二人新婚旅行從中國山海關西伯利亞世界最長
大[]道.當時要乘二週間到[經館].然後過英古到海峽到英
國看看就再乘船過大西洋到加拿大.　漫遊回來時自大西
洋經過巴拿馬連　河由台平洋回來台灣.回來了後就叫家
父取功讀牛律大學因為家父有讀過四書五經以及多多漢
文就聽從妹妹的.

P3

呼[叫]專心功讀牛律大學到畢業了.受派去八里教會牧會,
今再來講起.　阿姑婚後生育兒女一男張女嗎連嫁給陳清
義牧師.次女以利嫁給柯維思.男兒馬偕內廉是淡水中學創
設者.與本族加拿大女子給婚.　今來講起家父受派到八里
教會幾日久.當時家兄約伯出三歲學講話說出日本來了
騎馬連連請出二日.這也是上帝對小孩子開口來叫醒八里
教會柯維思幾位青年.事不知他們無有感覺在甲午載
爭[請]清將台灣[湮/斗]滿已割給日本統治　所以在台南請
武台官員.得着密命就偷冥乘船逃走回去大陸.　在台灣的
請兵無頭可管又是平時請兵無守軍欺負百性甚至拿民
家婦女去兵管無惠不作亡事仁多多.所以老百性順機會
來報復大家將淡水炮台火藥庫給百性功破也有八里柯維
斯幾位青年去運般十幾箱槍[器]子彈來放在禮拜堂廳的
双邊家父受派到八里也不知此事.　誅好觀音山頂出火号
有一隊抗日青年想要功人淡水日本軍官在那時候家兄約
伯上帝[]着 小孩口來提醒柯維思又幾位青年但是他們[]醒
果然日本陸軍步兵武裝二人入來禮拜堂叫家父連路入
拜堂廳双邊放在十幾箱槍[器]子彈家父也不知情行動自
然.在此危急時上帝大權能聖手來迷目二位日本兵無看
見双邊得箱只又看見門[楣]上一個空箱用槍尾力貯去.
声音是空箱就越過後面小厝外面出去.啊這宜在是主放落
大奇事神蹟來迷二位日本兵若無者我們一家一盡死在日
兵手下 若有我們一方存在世間大大感謝主的救恩到黃昏
時柯維思幾位青年透冥挖一大空來埋十幾箱槍器子彈.

Further reading 1b

Zhang Yuehan's account of the Early Church (translated by M. A. Dodge)

Zhang Yuehan's record on the power of the Lord manifested in through our family

April 1987, the 76th year of the Republic of China. May the Lord protect my humble family.

I originally come from Wugu Village (Go Kho-khi[n]). My grandfather Zhang Zhongsheng had three sons and one daughter. My father, Xintian (Sim Tiam) had one older brother and one younger brother. There was also a younger sister named Congzi (little onion). My aunt was thus given to be the daughter of another family. A while later, when she was twelve, her intended husband got sick and died. Her mother claimed that it was her witchlike manner that caused his sickness, and threatened to beat her to death. She would use any little excuse to punish her. One day, on New Year's Eve, her mother made her shell and peel two large buckets of dried peanuts (and potatoes) until her hands were cracked and in terrible pain. Then, on the 29th day of New Year's, there was nothing to eat for her except vegetable scraps. My mother told me that once there was a big rainstorm and Yangmu [adoptive mother] beat [Tiu[n]] fiercely, and she ran back to her birthmother's home in the middle of the night. When they answered the door, great aunt asked grandfather to crush up some medicine to give her before returning her to Yangmu's home. Great Aunt said that because the rain was so heavily, they ought to let her stay and take a bath and change her clothes. How could Grandfather take her back on such a night? There is no reason. He did not follow his master. He had no love for his own daughter. After she returned to her Yangmu's home every day she endured suffering that was too harsh to talk about. The day came when God blessed her family and protected her body and preserved her health. When she was fifteen, Dr Mackay first came to Taiwan to establish Oxford College and the clinic (now the Mackay Hospital) to treat people for pain, internal illnesses, and dental needs. He also came to teach students to preach at Oxford College. He recruited people both to train as medical assistants and preach the Gospel of Jesus Christ throughout the area. He set up a school in Go Kho-khiⁿ to teach boys and girls to read Taiwanese Vernacular in romanized letters (POJ) but after months, nobody came to the school. Later, Mackay promised a one silver dollar for boys and girls over the age of twelve who to come learn to read. At that time in the Qing Dynasty a whole bucket of rice only cost two cents. From the age of twelve, my aunt [Tiuⁿ] also studied there.

P2

More than a hundred people signed up to learn to read Taiwanese and learn to recite psalms and hymns to cultivate their hearts for the veneration of God. At the same time, it also preached the word of God to them. Of the hundreds of students who came, my aunt got the highest grade. After studying hard for some time everyone could read both the Old Testament and the New Testament, and Yangmu started being a little bit nicer to Tiuⁿ because she was able to earn money. After a while, Dr Mackay said that he would be going back to his mother country to report on the mission. Since transportation was not so convenient in those days, he would be gone a long time. It would be six months before he would return. When he returned he would give another test to see who could read a chapter of the New Testament the best. Each student would read one chapter. First prize would be three dollars, second prize two, and third prize one dollar. More than a hundred people came to compete, and my aunt read the best. She was very happy when she brought the prize back to her Yangmu. She was seventeen *sui* at this time. A student at Oxford College asked Mackay if he intended to assimilate (by intermarriage). He said yes. The student asked if he had determined who. Mackay answered, "Tiun Chhang because she is Chhang-miâ [brilliantly smart]". The student went directly to Tiuⁿ's Yangmu and asked if she would agree to let Mackay marry Tiuⁿ. Yangmu agreed. Dr Mackay offered a bride price of 30 silver dollars. He also promised that after they were married, she would receive three dollars a month until she was 100 sui. Dr Mackay used the Gospel of the Lord to change Tiuⁿ's Yangmu. She became a first-generation female believer in the Go Kho-khiⁿ church. Mackay changed her name when she was baptized. My aunt's name became Chhang-miâ. (Her wedding dress is still preserved in the Northern Synod's great meeting house.) After they were married the two left Shanhaiguan China and to Bolly on a westerly trip around the world. At that time it took two weeks to get to Jerusalem. Then they went through the Strait of Gibraltar to Britain and spent some time looking around there, then took a ship across the

Atlantic to Canada. When they returned home they crossed though the Panama Canal from the Atlantic Ocean and returned to Taiwan via the Pacific. When they returned [Tiuⁿ] invited my father to come study at Oxford College. Because he had studied the Four Books and the Five Classics and a lot of Han literature, he respected my sister's

P3

calling and decided to study there. He was assigned to the mission station at Bali, but I'll talk about that later. After she was married my aunt raised children. She had one son. The oldest daughter, Mary-Ellen, married Rev. Tan Ching-gi. The second daughter, Bella, married Koa Kau. The son, William Mackay, was the founder of Tamsui high school. He married a Canadian woman. Next let's talk about the time that my father was at the Bali Church. My eldest brother, Yuebo, who started talking when he was three, said he was going to Japan to ride horses for two days. This was also God speaking through the mouth of a babe to warn the young people of Bali. They did not know it yet, but the Qing Dynasty had ceded Taiwan to Japan. Taiwanese officials organized in the south to fight, but a secret order was given, and they all fled by boat to the mainland. In Taiwan there was no leader in charge of the army. There were no garrison times to organize and train them. Soldiers were coming around bullying hundreds of people. The people used every nice way to try to control the soldiers, even talking with the women from their families, but it did not work. So, the people took matters into their own hand and retaliated by destroying the arsenal at Tamsui. Ke Weisi and several young men from Bali were there, and they transported ten boxes of guns and ammunition to the Bali Church.

When my father was assigned to Bali, he did not know of this event. There was a group of anti-Japanese youth meeting on Guanyin Mountain and a Japanese Officer in Tamsui. God spoke through the voice of a child and awakened my brother Yuebo. Sure enough, two soldiers came and wanted to search the church, while there were twelve boxes of munitions hidden in it. My father didn't even know, he just acted naturally. At this critical moment God's almighty hand came to confuse the soldiers. They did not see the boxes lined up on either side of the chapel, just one box in the middle by the door. They hit the box with the butt of a gun, and it made an empty sound and fell over. They continued to the back of the church and left. It is a good thing that God wrought this great miracle to deceive these two soldiers, otherwise our family would have died at the hands of the Japanese soldiers. After that Ke Weisi and his group came and dug a great hole to bury the dozen boxes of munitions.

Further reading

Tiun Chhang-miâ's letter to Ma Yi-seng niang
(Transcribed and Translated to Mandarin and English by Robert Powei Young, Research Center, Presbyterian Church of Taiwan.)

加拿大，大英，正月 1881

Canada, Great Britain, January 1881. (CPC archives 2009-5004-1-10)

我所親愛的，馬醫師娘要予你知，我離開倫敦至今有惦記你們不止。我延遲寫，因為要寄給你我的相片。

My beloved, Mrs. Mackay would like you to know that I never ceased missing you all ever since I left London.

I wrote belatedly for I want to send you my pictures.

這裡的教會有頗思念台灣信心的人。每日下雪很高，水結冰，而人坐在木橇上，馬拖著也跑得快。

In the church here, there are lots of people who remember the faith in Taiwan dearly.

The snow falls high everyday and the water is frozen.

And when people sit on sleighs to be drawn by horses, they can run fast.

階牧師不在，因為每日到處、四處傳道。他頗想念你。今我問你們及孩子平安，上帝照顧你們。

Rev. Mackay is not present for he preaches everywhere, everyday. Now may peace be with you and the children.

May the Lord take care of you.

階聰明 筆

Written by Minnie Mackay

Index

www.ingramcontent.com/pod-product-compliance
Lightning Source LLC
Chambersburg PA
CBHW070329270326
41926CB00017B/3817